Techno-Nationalism and Techno-Globalism

Integrating National Economies: Promise and Pitfalls

Barry Bosworth (Brookings Institution) and Gur Ofer (Hebrew University)
Reforming Planned Economies in an Integrating World Economy

Ralph C. Bryant (Brookings Institution)
International Coordination of National Stabilization Policies

Susan M. Collins (Brookings Institution/Georgetown University)
Distributive Issues: A Constraint on Global Integration

Richard N. Cooper (Harvard University)
Environment and Resource Policies for the World Economy

Ronald G. Ehrenberg (Cornell University)
Labor Markets and Integrating National Economies

Barry Eichengreen (University of California, Berkeley)
International Monetary Arrangements for the 21st Century

Mitsuhiro Fukao (Bank of Japan)
Financial Integration, Corporate Governance, and the Performance of Multinational Companies

Stephan Haggard (University of California, San Diego)
Developing Nations and the Politics of Global Integration

Richard J. Herring (University of Pennsylvania) and Robert E. Litan (Department of Justice/Brookings Institution)
Financial Regulation in the Global Economy

Miles Kahler (University of California, San Diego)
International Institutions and the Political Economy of Integration

Anne O. Krueger (Stanford University)
Trade Policies and Developing Nations

Robert Z. Lawrence (Harvard University)
Regionalism, Multilateralism, and Deeper Integration

Sylvia Ostry (University of Toronto) and Richard R. Nelson (Columbia University)
Techno-Nationalism and Techno-Globalism: Conflict and Cooperation

Robert L. Paarlberg (Wellesley College/Harvard University)
Leadership Abroad Begins at Home: U.S. Foreign Economic Policy after the Cold War

Peter Rutland (Wesleyan University)
Russia, Eurasia, and the Global Economy

F. M. Scherer (Harvard University)
Competition Policies for an Integrated World Economy

Susan L. Shirk (University of California, San Diego)
How China Opened Its Door: The Political Success of the PRC's Foreign Trade and Investment Reforms

Alan O. Sykes (University of Chicago)
Product Standards for Internationally Integrated Goods Markets

Akihiko Tanaka (Institute of Oriental Culture, University of Tokyo)
The Politics of Deeper Integration: National Attitudes and Policies in Japan

Vito Tanzi (International Monetary Fund)
Taxation in an Integrating World

William Wallace (St. Antony's College, Oxford University)
Regional Integration: The West European Experience

Sylvia Ostry and
Richard R. Nelson

Techno-Nationalism and Techno-Globalism

Conflict and Cooperation

THE BROOKINGS INSTITUTION
Washington, D.C.

Copyright © 1995
THE BROOKINGS INSTITUTION
1775 Massachusetts Avenue, N. W., Washington, D. C. 20036

Library of Congress Cataloging-in-Publication data:
Ostry, Sylvia.
Techno-nationalism and techno-globalism: conflict and
cooperation / Sylvia Ostry and Richard R. Nelson.
p. cm. — (Integrating national economies)
Includes bibliographical references and index.
ISBN 0-8157-6674-2. — ISBN 0-8157-6673-4 (pbk.)
1. Technological innovations—Economic aspects—United States—
History—20th century. 2. Technological innovations—Economic
aspects—Japan—History—20th century. 3. Industries—United States—
History—20th century. 4. Industries—Japan—History—20th century.
5. Economic history—1945-   . 6. Competition, International—
History—20th century. I. Nelson, Richard R. II. Title.
HC110.T4082 1995
338′.064′0973—dc20   94-37871
                                                                CIP

9 8 7 6 5 4 3 2 1

The paper used in this publication meets the minimum requirements of
American National Standard for Information Sciences—Permanence of Paper
for Printed Library Materials, ANSI Z39.48-1984

Typeset in Plantin

Composition by Princeton Editorial Associates
Princeton, New Jersey

Printed by R. R. Donnelley and Sons Co.
Harrisonburg, Virginia

Foreword

*I*NTERNATIONAL economic policy increasingly affects domestic policy. The postwar Bretton Woods system, including the General Agreement on Tariffs and Trade, was designed to achieve a balance between a system of sustainable international rules governing trade and the ability of national governments to pursue their domestic economic objectives. In finance, these rules broke down in the early 1970s, and in trade too, international rules are intruding on domestic decisions more and more often. The Uruguay Round, launched in September 1986 and completed in December 1993, exemplifies this development in the service sector, intellectual property rights, technical barriers to trade, rules for investment, and even (or especially) agriculture.

This intrusion was especially evident during the 1980s in technology-intensive sectors, as high-tech firms became increasingly global. While explicit innovation policies are for the most part governed by the nation state, the policies, institutions, and behavior that affect the pace and nature of innovation are complex and defy national borders.

In this book the authors analyze this relationship between the globalism of firms and the nationalism of governments. They explore the interplay of cooperation and competition that characterizes high technology and propose some policy options to enhance global welfare and minimize friction.

Sylvia Ostry is chair of the Centre for International Studies at the University of Toronto. She is grateful to Geza Feketekuty, chairman of the OECD Trade Committee, Roger Heath of the Department of Industry, Science and Technology, Ottawa, and Deborah Wince-

Smith of the Council on Competitiveness. Richard Nelson is the George Blumenthal Professor of International and Public Affairs, Business, and Law at Columbia University. Both authors thank Robert Z. Lawrence for the invitation to participate in the Integrating National Economies project and are grateful for the helpful comments of the participants in the October 1993 review conference held at the Brookings Institution.

Princeton Editorial Associates edited the manuscript and prepared the index. Jeff McConnell verified the factual content of the manuscript. Sara C. Hufham prepared the reference list.

Funding for the project came from the Center for Global Partnership of the Japan Foundation, the Curry Foundation, the Ford Foundation, the Korea Foundation, the Tokyo Club Foundation for Global Studies, the United States-Japan Foundation, and the Alex C. Walker Educational and Charitable Foundation. The authors and Brookings are grateful for their support.

The views expressed in this book are those of the authors and should not be ascribed to any of the persons or organizations acknowledged above, or to the trustees, officers, or staff members of the Brookings Institution.

BRUCE K. MACLAURY
President

November 1994
Washington, D.C.

Contents

Figures

Preface to the Studies on Integrating National Economies

ECONOMIC interdependence among nations has increased sharply in the past half century. For example, while the value of total production of industrial countries increased at a rate of about 9 percent a year on average between 1964 and 1992, the value of the exports of those nations grew at an average rate of 12 percent, and lending and borrowing across national borders through banks surged upward even more rapidly at 23 percent a year. This international economic interdependence has contributed to significantly improved standards of living for most countries. Continuing international economic integration holds out the promise of further benefits. Yet the increasing sensitivity of national economies to events and policies originating abroad creates dilemmas and pitfalls if national policies and international cooperation are poorly managed.

The Brookings Project on Integrating National Economies, of which this study is a component, focuses on the interplay between two fundamental facts about the world at the end of the twentieth century. First, the world will continue for the foreseeable future to be organized politically into nation-states with sovereign governments. Second, increasing economic integration among nations will continue to erode differences among national economies and undermine the autonomy of national governments. The project explores the opportunities and tensions arising from these two facts.

Scholars from a variety of disciplines have produced twenty-one studies for the first phase of the project. Each study examines the heightened competition between national political sovereignty and increased cross-border economic integration. This preface identifies background themes and issues common to all the studies and provides a brief overview of the project as a whole.[1]

Increasing World Economic Integration

Two underlying sets of causes have led nations to become more closely intertwined. First, technological, social, and cultural changes have sharply reduced the effective economic distances among nations. Second, many of the government policies that traditionally inhibited cross-border transactions have been relaxed or even dismantled.

The same improvements in transportation and communications technology that make it much easier and cheaper for companies in New York to ship goods to California, for residents of Strasbourg to visit relatives in Marseilles, and for investors in Hokkaido to buy and sell shares on the Tokyo Stock Exchange facilitate trade, migration, and capital movements spanning nations and continents. The sharply reduced costs of moving goods, money, people, and information underlie the profound economic truth that technology has made the world markedly smaller.

New communications technology has been especially significant for financial activity. Computers, switching devices, and telecommunications satellites have slashed the cost of transmitting information internationally, of confirming transactions, and of paying for transactions. In the 1950s, for example, foreign exchange could be bought and sold only during conventional business hours in the initiating party's time zone. Such transactions can now be carried out instantaneously twenty-four hours a day. Large banks pass the management of their worldwide foreign-exchange positions around the globe from one branch to another, staying continuously ahead of the setting sun.

Such technological innovations have increased the knowledge of potentially profitable international exchanges and of economic opportunities abroad. Those developments, in turn, have changed consumers' and producers' tastes. Foreign goods, foreign vacations, foreign financial investments—virtually anything from other nations—have lost some of their exotic character.

---

1. A complete list of authors and study titles is included at the beginning of this volume, facing the title page.

Although technological change permits increased contact among nations, it would not have produced such dramatic effects if it had been countermanded by government policies. Governments have traditionally taxed goods moving in international trade, directly restricted imports and subsidized exports, and tried to limit international capital movements. Those policies erected "separation fences" at the borders of nations. From the perspective of private sector agents, separation fences imposed extra costs on cross-border transactions. They reduced trade and, in some cases, eliminated it. During the 1930s governments used such policies with particular zeal, a practice now believed to have deepened and lengthened the Great Depression.

After World War II, most national governments began—sometimes unilaterally, more often collaboratively—to lower their separation fences, to make them more permeable, or sometimes even to tear down parts of them. The multilateral negotiations under the auspices of the General Agreement on Trade and Tariffs (GATT)—for example, the Kennedy Round in the 1960s, the Tokyo Round in the 1970s, and most recently the protracted negotiations of the Uruguay Round, formally signed only in April 1994—stand out as the most prominent examples of fence lowering for trade in goods. Though contentious and marked by many compromises, the GATT negotiations are responsible for sharp reductions in at-the-border restrictions on trade in goods and services. After the mid-1980s a large number of developing countries moved unilaterally to reduce border barriers and to pursue outwardly oriented policies.

The lowering of fences for financial transactions began later and was less dramatic. Nonetheless, by the 1990s government restrictions on capital flows, especially among the industrial countries, were much less important and widespread than at the end of World War II and in the 1950s.

By shrinking the economic distances among nations, changes in technology would have progressively integrated the world economy even in the absence of reductions in governments' separation fences. Reductions in separation fences would have enhanced interdependence even without the technological innovations. Together, these two sets of evolutionary changes have reinforced each other and strikingly transformed the world economy.

Changes in the Government of Nations

Simultaneously with the transformation of the global economy, major changes have occurred in the world's political structure. First, the number of governmental decisionmaking units in the world has expanded markedly and political power has been diffused more broadly among them. Rising nationalism and, in some areas, heightened ethnic tensions have accompanied that increasing political pluralism.

The history of membership in international organizations documents the sharp growth in the number of independent states. For example, only 44 nations participated in the Bretton Woods conference of July 1944, which gave birth to the International Monetary Fund. But by the end of 1970, the IMF had 118 member nations. The number of members grew to 150 by the mid-1980s and to 178 by December 1993. Much of this growth reflects the collapse of colonial empires. Although many nations today are small and carry little individual weight in the global economy, their combined influence is considerable and their interests cannot be ignored as easily as they were in the past.

A second political trend, less visible but equally important, has been the gradual loss of the political and economic hegemony of the United States. Immediately after World War II, the United States by itself accounted for more than one-third of world production. By the early 1990s the U.S. share had fallen to about one-fifth. Concurrently, the political and economic influence of the European colonial powers continued to wane, and the economic significance of nations outside Europe and North America, such as Japan, Korea, Indonesia, China, Brazil, and Mexico, increased. A world in which economic power and influence are widely diffused has displaced a world in which one or a few nations effectively dominated international decisionmaking.

Turmoil and the prospect of fundamental change in the formerly centrally planned economies compose a third factor causing radical changes in world politics. During the era of central planning, governments in those nations tried to limit external influences on their economies. Now leaders in the formerly planned economies are trying to adopt reforms modeled on Western capitalist principles. To the extent that these efforts succeed, those nations will increase their economic involvement with the rest of the world. Political and economic alignments among the Western industrialized nations will be forced to adapt.

Governments and scholars have begun to assess these three trends, but their far-reaching ramifications will not be clear for decades.

Dilemmas for National Policies

Cross-border economic integration and national political sovereignty have increasingly come into conflict, leading to a growing mismatch between the economic and political structures of the world. The effective domains of economic markets have come to coincide less and less with national governmental jurisdictions.

When the separation fences at nations' borders were high, governments and citizens could sharply distinguish "international" from "domestic" policies. International policies dealt with at-the-border barriers, such as tariffs and quotas, or responded to events occurring abroad. In contrast, domestic policies were concerned with everything behind the nation's borders, such as competition and antitrust rules, corporate governance, product standards, worker safety, regulation and supervision of financial institutions, environmental protection, tax codes, and the government's budget. Domestic policies were regarded as matters about which nations were sovereign, to be determined by the preferences of the nation's citizens and its political institutions, without regard for effects on other nations.

As separation fences have been lowered and technological innovations have shrunk economic distances, a multitude of formerly neglected differences among nations' domestic policies have become exposed to international scrutiny. National governments and international negotiations must thus increasingly deal with "deeper"—behind-the-border—integration. For example, if country A permits companies to emit air and water pollutants whereas country B does not, companies that use pollution-generating methods of production will find it cheaper to produce in country A. Companies in country B that compete internationally with companies in country A are likely to complain that foreign competitors enjoy unfair advantages and to press for international pollution standards.

Deeper integration requires analysis of the economic and the political aspects of virtually all nonborder policies and practices. Such issues have already figured prominently in negotiations over the evolution of the European Community, over the Uruguay Round of GATT negotiations, over the North American Free Trade Agreement (NAFTA), and over the bilateral economic relationships between Japan and the United States. Future debates about behind-the-border policies will occur with increasing frequency and prove at least as complex and contentious as the past negotiations regarding at-the-border restrictions.

Tensions about deeper integration arise from three broad sources: cross-border spillovers, diminished national autonomy, and challenges to political sovereignty.

Cross-Border Spillovers

Some activities in one nation produce consequences that spill across borders and affect other nations. Illustrations of these spillovers abound. Given the impact of modern technology of banking and securities markets in creating interconnected networks, lax rules in one nation erode the ability of all other nations to enforce banking and securities rules and to deal with fraudulent transactions. Given the rapid diffusion of knowledge, science and technology policies in one nation generate knowledge that other nations can use without full payment. Labor market policies become matters of concern to other nations because workers migrate in search of work; policies in one nation can trigger migration that floods or starves labor markets elsewhere. When one nation dumps pollutants into the air or water that other nations breathe or drink, the matter goes beyond the unitary concern of the polluting nation and becomes a matter for international negotiation. Indeed, the hydrocarbons that are emitted into the atmosphere when individual nations burn coal for generating electricity contribute to global warming and are thereby a matter of concern for the entire world.

The tensions associated with cross-border spillovers can be especially vexing when national policies generate outcomes alleged to be competitively inequitable, as in the example in which country A permits companies to emit pollutants and country B does not. Or consider a situation in which country C requires commodities, whether produced at home or abroad, to meet certain design standards, justified for safety reasons. Foreign competitors may find it too expensive to meet these standards. In that event, the standards in C act very much like tariffs or quotas, effectively narrowing or even eliminating foreign competition for domestic producers. Citing examples of this sort, producers or governments in individual nations often complain that business is not conducted on a "level playing field." Typically, the complaining nation proposes that *other* nations adjust their policies to moderate or remove the competitive inequities.

Arguments for creating a level playing field are troublesome at best. International trade occurs precisely because of differences among nations—in resource endowments, labor skills, and consumer tastes. Nations specialize in producing goods and services in which they are relatively most efficient. In a fundamental sense, cross-border trade is valuable because the playing field is *not* level.

When David Ricardo first developed the theory of comparative advantage, he focused on differences among nations owing to climate or technology. But Ricardo could as easily have ascribed the productive differences to differing "social climates" as to physical or technological climates. Taking all "climatic" differences as given, the theory of comparative advantage argues that free trade among nations will maximize global welfare.

Taken to its logical extreme, the notion of leveling the playing field implies that nations should become homogeneous in all major respects. But that recommendation is unrealistic and even pernicious. Suppose country A decides that it is too poor to afford the costs of a clean environment, and will thus permit the production of goods that pollute local air and water supplies. Or suppose it concludes that it cannot afford stringent protections for worker safety. Country A will then argue that it is inappropriate for other nations to impute to country A the value they themselves place on a clean environment and safety standards (just as it would be inappropriate to impute the A valuations to the environment of other nations). The core of the idea of political sovereignty is to permit national residents to order their lives and property in accord with their own preferences.

Which perspective about differences among nations in behind-the-border policies is more compelling? Is country A merely exercising its national preferences and appropriately exploiting its comparative advantage in goods that are dirty or dangerous to produce? Or does a legitimate international problem exist that justifies pressure from other nations urging country A to accept changes in its policies (thus

curbing its national sovereignty)? When national governments negoti-
ate resolutions to such questions—trying to agree whether individual
nations are legitimately exercising sovereign choices or, alternatively,
engaging in behavior that is unfair or damaging to other nations—the
dialogue is invariably contentious because the resolutions depend on
the typically complex circumstances of the international spillovers
and on the relative weights accorded to the interests of particular
individuals and particular nations.

Diminished National Autonomy

As cross-border economic integration increases, governments experience greater difficulties in trying to control events within their
borders. Those difficulties, summarized by the term *diminished autonomy*, are the second set of reasons why tensions arise from the competition between political sovereignty and economic integration.

For example, nations adjust monetary and fiscal policies to influence domestic inflation and employment. In setting these policies,
smaller countries have always been somewhat constrained by foreign
economic events and policies. Today, however, all nations are constrained, often severely. More than in the past, therefore, nations may
be better able to achieve their economic goals if they work together
collaboratively in adjusting their macroeconomic policies.

Diminished autonomy and cross-border spillovers can sometimes
be allowed to persist without explicit international cooperation to
deal with them. States in the United States adopt their own tax
systems and set policies for assistance to poor single people without
any formal cooperation or limitation. Market pressures operate to
force a degree of de facto cooperation. If one state taxes corporations
too heavily, it knows business will move elsewhere. (Those familiar
with older debates about "fiscal federalism" within the United States
and other nations will recognize the similarity between those issues
and the emerging international debates about deeper integration of
national economies.) Analogously, differences among nations in regulations, standards, policies, institutions, and even social and cultural
preferences create economic incentives for a kind of arbitrage that
erodes or eliminates the differences. Such pressures involve not only
the conventional arbitrage that exploits price differentials (buying at
one point in geographic space or time and selling at another) but also

shifts in the location of production facilities and in the residence of factors of production.

In many other cases, however, cross-border spillovers, arbitrage pressures, and diminished effectiveness of national policies can produce unwanted consequences. In cases involving what economists call externalities (external economies and diseconomies), national governments may need to cooperate to promote mutual interests. For example, population growth, continued urbanization, and the more intensive exploitation of natural resources generate external diseconomies not only within but across national boundaries. External economies generated when benefits spill across national jurisdictions probably also increase in importance (for instance, the gains from basic research and from control of communicable diseases).

None of these situations is new, but technological change and the reduction of tariffs and quotas heighten their importance. When one nation produces goods (such as scientific research) or "bads" (such as pollution) that significantly affect other nations, individual governments acting sequentially and noncooperatively cannot deal effectively with the resulting issues. In the absence of explicit cooperation and political leadership, too few collective goods and too many collective bads will be supplied.

Challenges to Political Sovereignty

The pressures from cross-border economic integration sometimes even lead individuals or governments to challenge the core assumptions of national political sovereignty. Such challenges are a third source of tensions about deeper integration.

The existing world system of nation-states assumes that a nation's residents are free to follow their own values and to select their own political arrangements without interference from others. Similarly, property rights are allocated by nation. (The so-called global commons, such as outer space and the deep seabed, are the sole exceptions.) A nation is assumed to have the sovereign right to exploit its property in accordance with its own preferences and policies. Political sovereignty is thus analogous to the concept of consumer sovereignty (the presumption that the individual consumer best knows his or her own interests and should exercise them freely).

In times of war, some nations have had sovereignty wrested from them by force. In earlier eras, a handful of individuals or groups have questioned the premises of political sovereignty. With the profound increases in economic integration in recent decades, however, a larger number of individuals and groups—and occasionally even their national governments—have identified circumstances in which, it is claimed, some universal or international set of values should take precedence over the preferences or policies of particular nations.

Some groups seize on human-rights issues, for example, or what they deem to be egregiously inappropriate political arrangements in other nations. An especially prominent case occurred when citizens in many nations labeled the former apartheid policies of South Africa an affront to universal values and emphasized that the South African government was not legitimately representing the interests of a majority of South Africa's residents. Such views caused many national governments to apply economic sanctions against South Africa. Examples of value conflicts are not restricted to human rights, however. Groups focusing on environmental issues characterize tropical rain forests as the lungs of the world and the genetic repository for numerous species of plants and animals that are the heritage of all mankind. Such views lead Europeans, North Americans, or Japanese to challenge the timber-cutting policies of Brazilians and Indonesians. A recent controversy over tuna fishing with long drift nets that kill porpoises is yet another example. Environmentalists in the United States whose sensibilities were offended by the drowning of porpoises required U.S. boats at some additional expense to amend their fishing practices. The U.S. fishermen, complaining about imported tuna caught with less regard for porpoises, persuaded the U.S. government to ban such tuna imports (both direct imports from the countries in which the tuna is caught and indirect imports shipped via third countries). Mexico and Venezuela were the main countries affected by this ban; a GATT dispute panel sided with Mexico against the United States in the controversy, which further upset the U.S. environmental community.

A common feature of all such examples is the existence, real or alleged, of "psychological externalities" or "political failures." Those holding such views reject untrammeled political sovereignty for nation-states in deference to universal or non-national values. They wish to constrain the exercise of individual nations' sovereignties through international negotiations or, if necessary, by even stronger intervention.

The Management of International Convergence

In areas in which arbitrage pressures and cross-border spillovers are weak and psychological or political externalities are largely absent, national governments may encounter few problems with deeper integration. Diversity across nations may persist quite easily. But at the other extreme, arbitrage and spillovers in some areas may be so strong that they threaten to erode national diversity completely. Or psychological and political sensitivities may be asserted too powerfully to be ignored. Governments will then be confronted with serious tensions, and national policies and behaviors may eventually converge to common, worldwide patterns (for example, subject to internationally agreed norms or minimum standards). Eventual convergence across nations, if it occurs, could happen in a harmful way (national policies and practices being driven to a least common denominator with externalities ignored, in effect a "race to the bottom") or it could occur with mutually beneficial results ("survival of the fittest and the best").

Each study in this series addresses basic questions about the management of international convergence: if, when, and how national governments should intervene to try to influence the consequences of arbitrage pressures, cross-border spillovers, diminished autonomy, and the assertion of psychological or political externalities. A wide variety of responses is conceivable. We identify six, which should be regarded not as distinct categories but as ranges along a continuum.

National autonomy defines a situation at one end of the continuum in which national governments make decentralized decisions with little or no consultation and no explicit cooperation. This response represents political sovereignty at its strongest, undiluted by any international management of convergence.

Mutual recognition, like national autonomy, presumes decentralized decisions by national governments and relies on market competition to guide the process of international convergence. Mutual recognition, however, entails exchanges of information and consultations among governments to constrain the formation of national regulations and policies. As understood in discussions of economic integration within the European Community, moreover, mutual recognition entails an explicit acceptance by each member nation of the regulations, standards, and certification procedures of other members. For example, mutual recognition allows wine or liquor produced in any European Union country to be sold in all twelve member countries even if production standards in member countries differ. Doctors licensed in France are permitted to practice in Germany, and vice versa, even if licensing procedures in the two countries differ.

Governments may agree on rules that restrict their freedom to set policy or that promote gradual convergence in the structure of policy. As international consultations and monitoring of compliance with such rules become more important, this situation can be described as *monitored decentralization*. The Group of Seven finance ministers meetings, supplemented by the IMF's surveillance over exchange rate and macroeconomic policies, illustrate this approach to management.

Coordination goes further than mutual recognition and monitored decentralization in acknowledging convergence pressures. It is also more ambitious in promoting intergovernmental cooperation to deal with them. Coordination involves jointly designed mutual adjustments of national policies. In clear-cut cases of coordination, bargaining occurs and governments agree to behave differently from the ways they would have behaved without the agreement. Examples include the World Health Organization's procedures for controlling communicable diseases and the 1987 Montreal Protocol (to a 1985 framework convention) for the protection of stratospheric ozone by reducing emissions of chlorofluorocarbons.

Explicit harmonization, which requires still higher levels of intergovernmental cooperation, may require agreement on regional standards or world standards. Explicit harmonization typically entails still greater departures from decentralization in decisionmaking and still further strengthening of international institutions. The 1988 agreement among major central banks to set minimum standards for the required capital positions of commercial banks (reached through the Committee on Banking Regulations and Supervisory Practices at the Bank for International Settlements) is an example of partially harmonized regulations.

At the opposite end of the spectrum from national autonomy lies *federalist mutual governance*, which implies continuous bargaining and joint, centralized decisionmaking. To make federalist mutual governance work would require greatly strengthened supranational institutions. This end of the management spectrum, now relevant only as an analytical benchmark, is a possible outcome that can be imagined for the middle or late decades of the twenty-first century, possibly even sooner for regional groupings like the European Union.

Overview of the Brookings Project

Despite their growing importance, the issues of deeper economic integration and its competition with national political sovereignty were largely neglected in the 1980s. In 1992 the Brookings Institution initiated its project on Integrating National Economies to direct attention to these important questions.

In studying this topic, Brookings sought and received the co-operation of some of the world's leading economists, political scientists, foreign-policy specialists, and government officials, representing all regions of the world. Although some functional areas require a special focus on European, Japanese, and North American perspectives, at all junctures the goal was to include, in addition, the perspectives of developing nations and the formerly centrally planned economies.

The first phase of the project commissioned the twenty-one scholarly studies listed at the beginning of the book. One or two lead discussants, typically residents of parts of the world other than the area where the author resides, were asked to comment on each study.

Authors enjoyed substantial freedom to design their individual studies, taking due account of the overall themes and goals of the project. The guidelines for the studies requested that at least some of the analysis be carried out with a non-normative perspective. In effect, authors were asked to develop a "baseline" of what might happen in the absence of changed policies or further international cooperation. For their normative analyses, authors were asked to start with an agnostic posture that did not prejudge the net benefits or costs resulting from integration. The project organizers themselves had no presumption about whether national diversity is better or worse than international convergence or about what the individual studies should conclude regarding the desirability of increased integration. On the contrary, each author was asked to address the trade-offs in his or her issue area between diversity and convergence and to locate the area, currently and prospectively, on the spectrum of international management possibilities running between national autonomy through mutual recognition to coordination and explicit harmonization.

HENRY J. AARON   SUSAN M. COLLINS
RALPH C. BRYANT   ROBERT Z. LAWRENCE

Chapter 1

The Decline of American Hegemony and the Rise of Global Competition

*I*N THE QUARTER CENTURY after World War II, the United States was the world's dominant technological and economic power. That lead has eroded significantly over the past twenty years. An important reason has been the great increase in international trade, investment, and technology that has occured over this period. With the globalization of business and competition, particularly in the field of high technology, considerable debate has arisen within and across nations concerning the fairness and productiveness of public policy in this field. The issues at the heart of these disputes are the subject of this book.

No discussion of the issues can proceed very far, however, without examining the changing position of the United States in the world economic and technological order. At the end of World War II, Americans were at the center of the stage and expected to remain there for some time to come. In contrast, Japan then was a poor country, and most of its firms were far behind those of both Europe and the United States. Needless to say, Japan's rise as a technological and economic power came as a great surprise. Americans and Europeans alike looked at what happened and concluded that someone—primarily Japan—must have cheated or done something unfair. The Japanese countered that their economic success was a just reward for hard work, high rates of saving and investment, and sound economic policies.

In the past several years there have been signs that the United States had perhaps been written off too soon and that Japanese prowess was blown out of proportion. Price deflators based on pur-

1

chasing power parity suggest that the United States continues to have a higher per capita income than Japan, as well as higher productivity levels across a wide range of industries. The American automobile and semiconductor industries, which appeared to be in serious decline, have made strong comebacks. At the same time, economic growth in Japan has slowed drastically. Whether this is a new trend or simply the swing of a cycle is not yet clear. What seems indisputable, however, is that American technological dominance is gone, probably for good.

The Rise and Erosion of American Technological Leadership

In the 1950s and 1960s, the United States had a distinct technological advantage in two broad areas of manufacturing: mass production, particularly of automobiles, steel, and consumer durables; and high technology, notably in electronics, aerospace, and pharmaceuticals, which were the new industries of the era.[1]

The United States advantage in mass production came into place toward the end of the nineteenth century, and the United States lead was commanding by World War I.[2] Around the turn of the century American worker productivity and per capita income surged past that in Great Britain and far beyond the levels on the European continent.[3] At that time, Japan was a poor and technologically backward nation. Because of the large size of the American market, U.S. industries such as steel and automobiles were able to take advantage of economies of scale and thus had a higher output per worker than their British and European counterparts. The capital intensity of American industry was also significantly greater, as were real wages.

More generally, by that time the United States had become the world's largest and richest common market. By World War I, its total gross national product (GNP) was more than double that of Great Britain, not only because of its larger population and higher incomes but also its higher productivity. In the economic world at that time, and indeed up until the Bretton Woods agreement and General Agreement on Tariffs and Trade (GATT) after World War II, firms strongly favored access to their home market, and there were many

1. This section follows the lines drawn in Nelson and Wright (1992, pp. 1931–64).
2. Chandler and Hikino (1990).
3. See Maddison (1991).

obstacles to trade. Although American firms catered by and large to the domestic market, many quickly became dominant exporters because of their efficiency advantages. Thus, after 1913 and right up until the beginning of World War II, the United States was by far the world's largest exporter of motor vehicles.[4] American firms also dominated world markets in a wide range of consumer durables that had come into existence in the interwar period, such as refrigerators and vacuum cleaners.

In contrast, the American lead in high-technology products did not appear until after World War II. That was when the American strength in basic science blossomed, as is evident from the marked increase in Nobel prizes in physics and chemistry awarded to American scientists after 1950 (figure 1-1). By the early 1960s the United States was the world's leader in science and in industries linked to science, such as electronics and pharmaceuticals.

Among the reasons for this surge was the growing number of young Americans entering the work force who had college degrees in science or engineering and the increase in research and development (R&D) spending as a fraction of GNP. The United States stood far ahead of Europe on these variables (see figures 1-2 and 1-3). In 1969 total U.S. expenditure on R&D was more than double that in the United Kingdom, Germany, France, and Japan combined.

Industrial R&D received heavy inflows of both private and public investment. Pharmaceutical and chemical firms received most of their R&D financing from the private sector, whereas those producing equipment for the military and space agencies relied almost entirely on government funding. Both private and public funds went into R&D in fields such as telecommunications, computers, semiconductors, and large aircraft, the products of which could be tailored either to a military or a civilian market.

Perhaps because they were accustomed to American productivity and technological dominance in the steel and automobile industries, the Europeans were primarily concerned about American domination in such fields as semiconductors, computers, telecommunications, and jet aircraft.[5] Thus in the mid-1960s the Organisation for Eco-

---

4. Nelson and Wright (1992, p. 1945).

5. For a discussion of European concerns in the mid-1960s, see Servan-Schreiber (1968, p. 101).

Figure 1-1. *Cumulative Nobel Prizes in Physics and Chemistry, 1901–90*

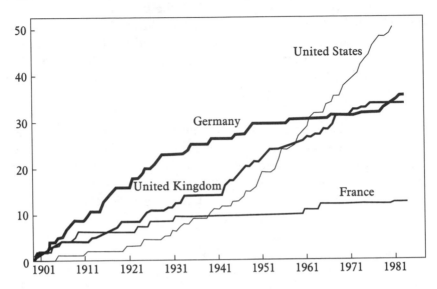

Source: Authors' tabulations. See World Almanac (1993, pp. 300–01).

nomic Co-operation and Development issued a series of reports assessing the magnitude of the "technological gap" and the factors behind it. Interestingly, just at the time that European alarm and American complacency were at their greatest, the United States was beginning to lose its lead, both in the aggregate and in individual fields, to Europe and Japan. The convergence in productivity is clearly shown in figure 1-4. The rise of Japan as a major exporter stands out in table 1-1.

One central reason for convergence was undoubtedly the lowering of barriers to the flow of trade, investment, and technology. Between the 1960s and the 1980s, U.S. imports as a fraction of GNP almost tripled (table 1-2). Over the same period, the ratio of imports to GNP in France, Germany, Italy, and the United Kingdom taken as a group increased by about 50 percent. It grew by a third in Japan until the early 1980s but then declined significantly. The highest increases were recorded for manufacturing, for it was in this area in particular that efficient companies producing attractive products had succeeded in

Figure 1-2. *Number of Scientists and Engineers Engaged in R&D,
per 10,000 workers, 1965, 1972, 1981, and 1987*

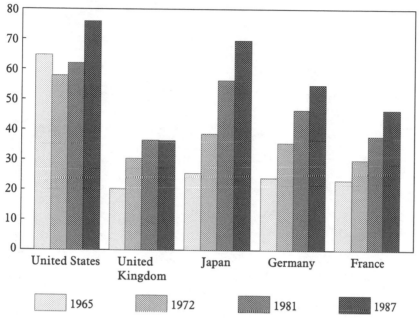

Source: National Science Board (1989 and 1991, appendix table 3-19).

entering world markets. The advantage of mass production that had
for many years given American firms more or less exclusive access to
the world's largest market had disappeared. Despite some fear of a
return to protectionism, by the 1980s much of the world had become
a common market.

In this new environment, more and more business was conducted on a transnational level. Certainly, many American companies had long had branches in Europe. However, the scale of
American overseas direct investment expanded dramatically in the
1950s and 1960s. By the late 1960s, however, Europe was establishing branches or buying plants in the United States, and in
recent years Japanese companies have done the same on a very
large scale (see chapter 2).

Figure 1-3. *Expenditures on Research and Development as a Percentage of GNP, 1964, 1971, 1978, 1989*

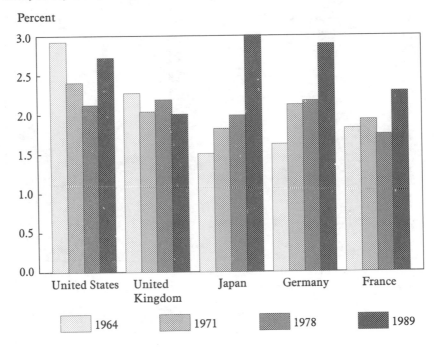

Source: National Science Board (1989, appendix table 4-19; 1991, appendix table 4-26).

This internationalization of trade and business has eroded national barriers to the transfer of technology. In the early postwar period, American firms clearly knew how to do things that firms based in other countries did not. Only a small part of what one needed to know to be an efficient producer of steel or automobiles or radios was published in books or taught in engineering schools. Rather, most of it had to be learned through experience. Moreover, American firms were not operating in the same kind of market or employing the same technologies as European and Japanese firms.

The situation now is quite different. Since World War II a great deal of progress has been made in understanding the scientific basis of most industrial technologies, and that knowledge is more readily accessible in scientific and engineering training programs and in

Figure 1-4. *Gross Domestic Product per Hour, 1870–1986*

Log scale

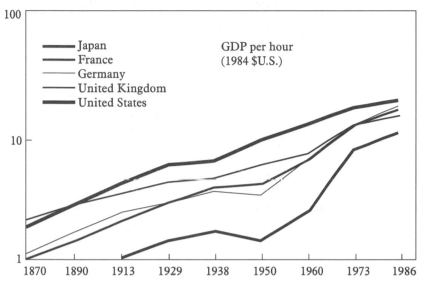

Source: Maddison (1991, pp. 274–275, table C.11).

widely available publications.[6] Also, the markets firms face in different countries have become more and more similar, and their operations no longer differ to any significant extent.

Formal training in science and engineering has therefore become essential to gaining command over industrial technology. At the same time, formal research and development programs have become the primary means by which companies design, debug, and gain initial mastery over new products and processes. Although a great deal of effort has gone into the codification of generic scientific knowledge, firms still need to invest an enormous amount of time in designing and learning to produce a specific product or in learning to master a sophisticated production process. These investments are large enough if a company simply wants to keep up with a rapidly evolving technology. Far more is required to be a leader. Recognizing that they would need to make massive investments in education and R&D to catch up

6. There has been an enormous increase alone in the number of scientific articles cited by patents. See Narin and Noma (1985, pp. 369–81).

Table 1-1. *Share of Triad Exports by Technological Category, 1966–91*
Percent

Year	Total	Low	Medium	High
United States				
1966	22	20	22	25
1978	23.1	24.8	21.3	25.2
1982	24.9	24.2	23.0	28.6
1986	20.0	17.4	17.0	25.9
1990	21.3	19.4	18.5	26.0
1991	21.8	19.5	19.3	26.0
Newly industrializing economies of Asia				
1966	1	1	0	0
1978	5.5	8.3	2.0	5.9
1982	7.5	10.4	3.0	8.6
1986	8.5	12.6	3.9	10.5
1990	10.9	14.8	5.4	14.3
1991	11.9	16.2	6.2	15.0
France, Germany, Italy, and the United Kingdom				
1966	70	71	71	66
1978	55.7	55.6	60.0	44.1
1982	51.4	53.0	55.1	39.0
1986	52.2	59.7	56.0	38.3
1990	52.2	58.5	57.7	36.8
1991	50.1	56.6	55.1	35.9
Japan				
1966	7	8	7	9
1978	15.7	11.3	16.7	24.9
1982	16.3	12.3	18.9	23.7
1986	19.3	10.3	23.1	25.3
1990	15.6	7.3	18.4	22.9
1991	16.2	7.6	19.4	23.1

Source: United Nations, *International Trade Statistics Yearbook*, various issues; technology categories based on categorization used in OECD (1992b, p. 152).

with the United States, the other industrial nations poured a great deal of effort into these activities from the mid-1960s on (see figures 1-2 and 1-3). Thus by the mid-1980s they had narrowed the American lead in scientists and engineers as a fraction of the workforce and in R&D as a fraction of GNP.

Table 1-2. *Imports as a Share of GDP in Prominent Industrialized Countries, 1963–92*
Percent

Country	1963–67	1968–72	1973–77	1978–82	1983–87	1988–92
United States	3.1	4.0	6.6	8.3	8.4	8.9
Japan	7.7	7.2	9.9	10.4	8.2	6.5
EC Big Four[a]	12.4	13.8	17.9	20.1	20.1	18.2
Average	7.8	8.4	11.5	12.9	12.2	11.2

Source: IMF (1993), for the United States, pp. 724–27; for Japan, pp. 440–41; for Germany, pp. 366–69; for the United Kingdom, pp. 720–21; for France, pp. 354–55, for Italy, pp. 432–33.

a. Average of shares: France, Germany, the United Kingdom, and Italy.

The United States, however, continued to be by far the largest investor in military R&D. Whereas during the 1950s and 1960s that dominance in new military technology gave the United States significant advantages in civilian technology, today it buys little outside the military sphere. Its access to this technology has little effect on productivity in industry as a whole and thus does not hurt the Europeans or the Japanese.

Several recent studies have explained at some length why military R&D has become less important to civilian technology, and thus there is no need to cover that topic here.[7] In all likelihood, the amount of R&D effort that goes into military programs will be greatly reduced in the coming years, as the Clinton administration has proposed (see chapter 2).

The important point is that these various developments have brought the industrial nations closer together in technological competence than was the case even twenty years ago. Of course it is still possible for a company or small group of companies to dominate a particular area of technology, at least for a certain period of time. And it is also possible for those companies to be concentrated in one country. Japanese companies today dominate memory chips, for example, and American ones dominate microprocessors. But the gaps in competence are likely to be much smaller and of shorter duration than they used to be, although the investments needed to maintain one's lead may be very large.

Also because of these developments high-technology industries now compete on different terms, and firms have drastically changed

7. For a recent review, see Alic and others (1992).

their organization and business strategy. American firms can no longer merely concern themselves with their domestic rivals, as they did
under the old system of oligopolistic "fair" competition with each
other or with their rivals in Europe. Now they face strong competition, from Japan and the Asian "tigers."

With the increase in international trade in manufactured products,
more firms have become "multinational" entities that conduct a
significant share of their business outside their home country. In
addition, in recent years there has been a significant increase in
contractual cooperative relationships between firms of different home
nationalities.

Globalization during the 1980s: The Onset of Technoglobalism

This interdependence spread throughout the world's financial markets in the 1970s, to give rise in the 1980s to the so-called globalization. Its principal characteristics were an unprecedented increase in
foreign direct investment; greatly intensified international rivalry, especially among the technologically advanced industries; and greater
trade liberalization, following successive rounds of multilateral negotiations in the GATT. These changes in both trade and investment
patterns facilitated the diffusion of technology, especially from the
dominant technological power, the United States. As other countries
acquired new technologies and became more competitive the United
States lost increasing ground. At the same time, it almost tripled its
share of imports after 1960.

The steady increase in trade flows over the past three decades has
been accompanied by a significant change in the *sectoral composition* of
trade, from low-tech to high-tech goods, especially in the developed
economies. The share of low-technology goods in manufacturing
exports declined from 45 percent in the mid-1960s to about 35 percent at the end of the 1980s, whereas the share of high-tech categories
rose from 16 to 24 percent. Medium-tech goods maintained roughly
the same share over this period.

The great concern for the United States, as already mentioned, was
that this high-tech trade was moving out of its sphere of control.
Europe, too, saw its share of the trade plummet over the 1980s, and

even Japan experienced a decline it its share of high-tech exports in the second half of the 1980s (table 1-1). In contrast, the newly industrializing economies of Asia found their comparative advantage had increased dramatically (table 1-3). As a result, many of the developed countries decided to revamp their trade and domestic policies, as explained in the following chapters.

The trends behind these changing trade flows are not entirely clear from U.S. *trade balances* in manufacturing (table 1-4), however, because of the extreme exchange rate swings of the 1980s.[8] Much of the decline in the high-tech trade balance in the first half of the 1980s was due to the overvalued dollar, and the improvement that began after the Plaza Accord of 1985 reflects the devaluation launched at that time. Nonetheless, the erosion of the U.S. lead, the remarkable increase in Japan's high-tech trade balance, and the declining position of the Europeans are clearly evident over the longer haul (see figure 1-5). Rising import penetration rather than the declining export share accounts for the erosion of the U.S. trade balance (table 1-5). The contrast with Japan in this respect is especially striking.

Another significant development linked with the growth of technology-intensive manufacturing, especially in the industrialized countries, has been the increase in *intraindustry trade,* that is, trade within the same broad industry or product group (table 1-6). This trade pattern reflects increasing specialization by oligopolistic firms and also increasing foreign investment by these firms in each other's home markets. The OECD countries account for more than 85 percent of all trade in high- and medium-intensity R&D manufacturing, and oligopolistic rivalry in these sectors is fierce in both home and foreign markets.[9]

Much of the intraindustry trade also takes place within multinational firms, between the parent and its subsidiaries or among the subsidiaries. Unfortunately, little information is available on this important aspect of interdependence, except for some statistics from the United States and Japan.[10] In 1989, for example, nearly 40 percent of United States merchandise exports and more than two-fifths of its merchandise imports were intrafirm transactions (see tables 1-7 and

---

8. See, for example, Krugman (1992).
9. Kurth (1992, p. 22, table 5).
10. OECD (1993a).

Table 1-3. *Revealed Comparative Advantage of the Leading Industrialized Economies, 1966–91*

Year	Low	Medium	High
United States			
1966	0.92	1.01	1.15
1978	1.07	0.92	1.09
1982	0.98	0.92	1.15
1986	0.87	0.85	1.29
1990	0.91	0.87	1.22
1991	0.90	0.89	1.20
Japan			
1966	1.09	0.94	1.24
1978	0.72	1.07	1.59
1982	0.76	1.16	1.46
1986	0.54	1.20	1.32
1990	0.47	1.18	1.47
1991	0.47	1.20	1.42
The EC Big Four[a]			
1966	0.93	1.04	0.95
1978	1.06	1.03	0.76
1982	1.09	1.02	0.74
1986	1.21	1.01	0.72
1990	1.18	1.05	0.69
1991	1.18	1.06	0.70
The NICs[b]			
1966	1.59	0.38	0.44
1978	1.48	0.37	1.06
1982	1.39	0.41	1.16
1986	1.40	0.45	1.26
1990	1.30	0.49	1.36
1991	1.29	0.50	1.32

Source: United Nations, *International Trade Statistics Yearbook,* various issues; trade classification based on OECD (1992b, box 14, p. 152).

Note: Revealed comparative advantage is the ratio of the share of a given category's exports in a given country's total exports over the share of the same category's exports for all the countries in the sample.

a. France, Germany, Italy, and the United Kingdom.

b. Hong Kong, Korea, Singapore, and Taiwan.

Table 1-4. *U.S. Trade Ratios (Exports over Imports) by Technological Category, 1966–91*

Year	Total	Low	Medium	High
1966	1.17	0.80	2.17	2.28
1978	0.78	0.84	1.10	1.52
1982	0.83	0.86	1.09	1.53
1986	0.56	0.49	0.54	0.88
1990	0.76	0.68	0.80	1.13
1991	0.83	0.72	0.88	1.16

Source: United Nations, *International Trade Statistics Yearbook*, various years.
Note: The technology classification system used here is based on OECD (1992b, box 14, p. 152).

Figure 1-5. *Trade Balance in High-Technology Manufactures for Selected OECD Countries*

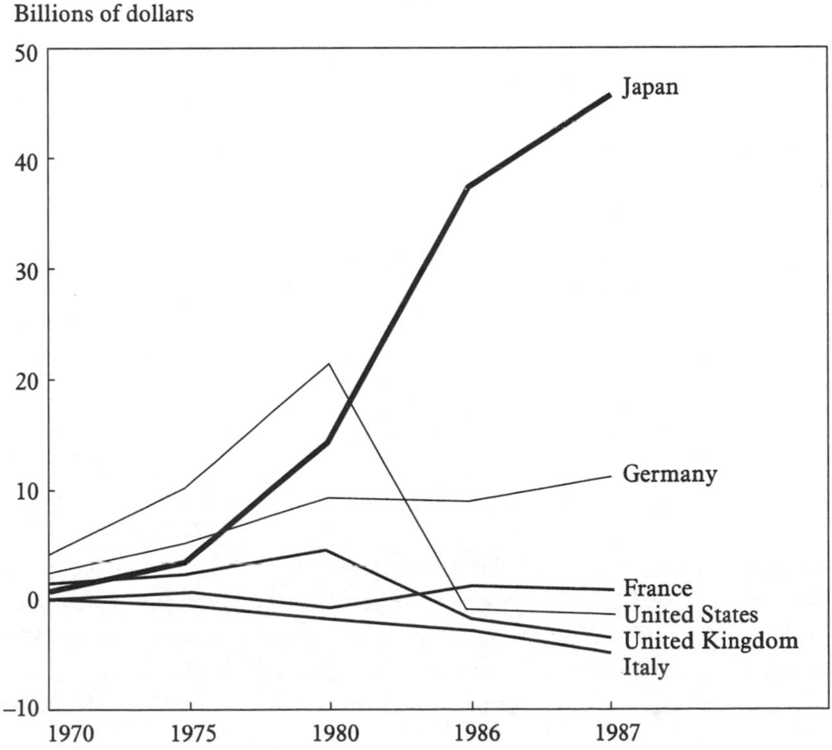

Billions of dollars

Source: OECD (1992c, p. 24).

Table 1-5. *Export Shares, Revealed Comparative Advantage, and Import Penetration in the Developed Economies, 1970 and 1990*

Country	Technology level	Export shares[a]		Revealed comparative advantage[b]		Import penetration[c]	
		1970	1990	1970	1990	1970	1990
United States	High	31.1	26.3	1.54	1.51	4.2	18.4
	Medium	21.7	15.4	1.07	0.89	5.6	18.5
	Low	13.4	13.3	0.66	0.76	3.8	8.8
Japan	High	13.2	21.1	1.20	1.41	5.2	5.4
	Medium	8.5	16.9	0.77	1.12	4.5	5.9
	Low	13.2	7.1	1.19	0.47	3.0	6.6
Germany	High	17.7	16.2	0.93	0.79	14.9	37.0
	Medium	23.1	24.7	1.22	1.20	17.2	29.5
	Low	15.0	17.9	0.79	0.87	11.1	20.9
France	High	7.7	8.7	0.83	0.84	21.6	31.6
	Medium	8.5	10.0	0.92	0.97	19.7	34.1
	Low	10.7	12.1	1.15	1.18	10.7	21.4
Italy	High	5.5	5.1	0.75	0.59	16.2	22.8
	Medium	7.1	7.7	0.97	0.89	23.6	28.9
	Low	8.5	12.8	1.16	1.49	11.6	15.7
United Kingdom	High	10.5	10.2	1.01	1.16	17.4	42.4
	Medium	11.9	8.5	1.14	0.96	n.a.	39.4
	Low	8.9	8.5	0.85	0.95	12.4	19.8
EC 6[d]	High	37.8	32.8	0.90	0.82	n.a.	n.a.
	Medium	45.3	43.7	1.03	1.01	n.a.	n.a.
	Low	40.8	48.5	1.01	1.13	n.a.	n.a.

Source: OECD (1993c, p. 87, table 16).

n.a.: not available

a. Share of OECD exports in each category.

b. Revealed comparative advantage is calculated as a country's export in an industry divided by its total exports normalized by the same ratio for the OECD countries.

c. Imports divided by total domestic demand (production plus imports less exports).

d. Germany, France, Italy, United Kingdom, the Netherlands, and Denmark.

1-8). The ratios for such transactions are highest in high-wage, technology-intensive sectors such as machinery, electronic equipment, and transportation equipment. Regression analysis indicates that R&D intensity is the most important determinant of intrafirm exports and imports.[11] These ratios declined in the first half of the 1980s, probably

11. Siddharthan and Kumar (1990, pp. 581–90), cited in OECD (1993a, pp. 29–30).

Table 1-6. *Bilateral Intraindustry Trade Indices, Total Products, for the G-7 Countries, Selected Years*

Country	Year	Japan	Germany	France	United Kingdom
United States	1970	32	44	52	52
	1980	31	48	59	55
	1990	48	64	69	63
Japan	1970		54	62	45
	1980		69	47	66
	1990		77	31	62
Germany	1970			72	77
	1980			83	59
	1990			88	76
France	1970				66
	1980				69
	1990				81
United Kingdom	1970				
	1980				
	1990				

Source: OECD (1992b, pp. 206–09).

Note: Intraindustry trade (IIT) is a measure of two-way trade within the same industrial or product classification. As an example of intraindustry trade, Japan exports laptop computers to the United States, while the United States exports mainframe computers to Japan. For a particular product or industry i, IIT is defined as the value of total trade $(Xi + Mi)$ remaining after subtraction of the absolute value of net exports or imports, $|Xi - Mi|$. In order to be able to compare trade between countries and industries, the measure is expressed as a percentage of each industry's combined exports and imports. A measure of *inter*industry trade is then expressed as $100[|Xi - Mi|/(Xi + Mi)]$ and the *intra*industry trade measure is given by $100(1 - [|Xi - Mi|/(Xi + Mi)])$. The index varies between 0 and 100. If a country exports and imports roughly equal quantities of a certain product, the IIT index is high. If it is mainly one-way trade (whether exporting or importing), the IIT index is low. For aggregation purposes, the measure can be summed over many industries. Figures are calculated from SITC Rev. 2, three-digit product categories, and are adjusted for overall trade imbalances.

because of the impact of the appreciation of the dollar. Since the information on Japan is less detailed, it is difficult to carry out a meaningful comparison, except to point out that wholesale trade accounts for 36 percent of intrafirm exports and 72 percent of intrafirm imports in Japan (tables 1-9 and 1-10).[12] Also, there is a higher concentration of intrafirm trade in technology-intensive sectors in Japan than in the United States.

In 1988 more than 80 percent of U.S. trade was conducted by multinational enterprises. In 1989 their sales as a whole (that is, worldwide sales of their foreign affiliates in host countries, which

12. See Yamawaki (1991, pp. 294–300).

Table 1-7. U.S. Merchandise Exports Shipped by U.S. Parents, by Industry of Parent, Selected Years
Millions of dollars and percentage

Industry	U.S. exports shipped by U.S. parents		Exports shipped to U.S. foreign affiliates		Intrafirm export ratio[a]		
	1989	Share	1989	Share	1989	1982	1977
All industries	228,576	100.0	89,151	100.0	39.0	30.4	34.7
Manufacturing	183,510	80.3	81,597	91.5	44.5	38.1	41.9
Food and kindred products	9,828	4.3	1,589	1.8	16.2	18.6	21.9
Chemicals	24,406	10.7	11,709	13.1	48.0	36.2	45.0
Primary and fabricated metals	7,381	3.2	1,582	1.8	21.4	16.4	24.1
Machinery, except electrical	36,781	16.1	22,535	25.3	61.3	51.1	42.1
Electric and electronic equipment	19,907	8.7	7,355	8.3	36.9	32.4	34.5
Transportation equipment	57,793	25.3	27,890	31.3	48.3	42.8	50.2
Other manufacturing	27,414	12.0	8,936	10.0	32.6	35.7	40.1
Wholesale and retail trade	30,191	13.2	2,788	3.1	9.2	11.5	9.0
Petroleum and related products	9,749	4.3	3,099	3.5	31.8	14.5	36.3

Source: OECD (1993a, p. 38).
a. Intrafirm export ratio is defined as the share of exports shipped to U.S. foreign affiliates in total exports shipped by U.S. parents.

Table 1-8. *U.S. Merchandise Imports Shipped to U.S. Parents, by Industry of Parent, Selected Years*
Millions of dollars and percentage

Industry	U.S. imports shipped to U.S. parents		Of which shipped by U.S. foreign affiliates		Intrafirm import ratio[a]		
	1989	Share	1989	Share	1989	1982	1977
All industries	174,874	100.0	75,984	100.0	43.5	37.5	41.9
Manufacturing	105,753	60.5	62,283	82.0	58.9	62.4	56.1
Food and kindred products	3,556	2.0	996	1.3	28.0	21.8	n.a.
Chemicals	11,091	6.3	3,783	5.0	34.1	n.a.	35.4
Primary and fabricated metals	5,305	3.0	1,885	2.5	35.5	n.a.	38.5
Machinery, except electrical	17,026	9.7	12,789	16.8	75.1	74.2	58.6
Electric and electronic equipment	12,956	7.4	5,332	7.0	41.2	53.9	60.3
Transportation equipment	45,380	26.0	31,919	42.0	70.3	n.a.	n.a.
Other manufacturing	10,439	6.0	5,579	7.3	53.4	43.3	42.1
Wholesale and retail trade	39,566	22.6	3,879	5.1	9.8	n.a.	11.1
Petroleum and related products	25,681	14.7	7,346	9.7	28.6	21.5	39.7

Source: OECD (1993a, p. 39).

n.a.: Not available.

a. Intrafirm import ratio is defined as the share of imports shipped by U.S. foreign affiliates in total imports shipped to U.S. parents.

Table 1-9. *Sales and Exports Associated with Japanese Multinational Enterprises, by Industry of Parent, Fiscal 1989*
Billions of yen and percentage

Industry	(1) Total sales by Japanese parents		(2) Total exports shipped by Japanese parents		(3) Exports shipped to Japanese foreign affiliates		(4) Export sales ratio (2)/(1)	(5) Intrafirm export ratio (3)/(2)
	Value	*Share*	*Value*	*Share*	*Value*	*Share*		
All industries	315,548	100.0	47,560	100.0	15,533	100.0	15.1	32.7
Manufacturing	125,004	39.6	24,121	50.7	9,912	63.8	19.3	41.1
Food and beverages	8,413	2.7	63	0.1	12	0.1	0.7	19.0
Textiles	1,883	0.6	122	0.3	4	0.0	6.5	3.3
Wood and paper products	2,130	0.7	104	0.2	5	0.0	4.9	4.8
Chemicals	10,742	3.4	1,004	2.1	220	1.4	9.3	21.9
Iron and steel	8,006	2.5	1,548	3.3	22	0.1	19.3	1.4
Nonferrous metals	4,234	1.3	295	0.6	57	0.4	7.0	19.3
General machinery	6,090	1.9	1,364	2.9	597	3.8	22.4	43.8
Electrical machinery	30,658	9.7	7,876	16.6	4,008	25.8	25.7	50.9
Transport equipment	31,921	10.1	8,857	18.6	3,639	23.4	27.7	41.1
Precision instruments	2,755	0.9	1,031	2.2	544	3.5	37.4	52.8
Petroleum and coal products	7,380	2.3	124	0.3	45	0.3	1.7	36.3
Other manufacturing	10,813	3.4	1,734	3.6	759	4.9	16.0	43.8
Wholesale and retail trade	159,502	50.5	22,894	48.1	5,596	36.0	14.4	24.4

Source: OECD (1993a, p.51).

Note: A Japanese multinational enterprise consists of a Japanese parent (excluding finance, insurance, and real estate industries) and its foreign affiliates. A Japanese parent is a Japanese person who owns or controls 10 percent or more of voting securities of an incorporated foreign business enterprise. Japanese foreign affiliates consist of (1) foreign subsidiaries so controlled by Japanese parents, and (2) foreign business enterprises that are more than 50 percent owned by the majority-owned Japanese foreign subsidiaries ("grandchildren"). The MITI benchmark survey does not provide estimates of the whole universe so that these data are not strictly comparable with those provided by U.S. Department of Commerce, Benchmark Survey.

Table 1-10. *Procurement and Imports Associated with Japanese Multinational Enterprises by Industry of Parent, Fiscal 1989*
Billions of yen and percentage

	(1) Total procurement by Japanese parents		(2) Total imports shipped to Japanese parents		(3) Imports shipped by Japanese foreign affiliates		(4) Import sales ratio	(5) Intrafirm import ratio
Industry	Value	Share	Value	Share	Value	Share	(2)/(1)	(3)/(2)
All industries	258,626	100.0	38,752	100.0	11,128	100.0	15.0	28.7
Manufacturing	78,201	30.2	9,823	25.3	3,037	27.3	12.6	30.9
Food and beverages	4,558	1.8	525	1.4	77	0.7	11.5	14.7
Textiles	969	0.4	159	0.4	24	0.2	16.4	15.1
Wood and paper products	1,505	0.6	328	0.8	75	0.7	21.8	22.9
Chemicals	4,415	1.7	468	1.2	46	0.4	10.6	9.8
Iron and steel	3,869	1.5	932	2.4	5	0.0	24.1	0.5
Nonferrous metals	3,023	1.2	616	1.6	35	0.3	20.4	5.7
General machinery	3,333	1.3	92	0.2	31	0.3	2.8	33.7
Electrical machinery	20,314	7.9	2,173	5.6	779	7.0	10.7	35.8
Transport equipment	22,295	8.6	1,696	4.4	610	5.5	7.6	36.0
Precision instruments	1,789	0.7	97	0.3	37	0.3	5.4	38.1
Petroleum and coal products	6,353	2.5	2,363	6.1	1,223	11.0	37.2	51.8
Other manufacturing	5,779	2.2	375	1.0	94	0.8	6.5	25.1
Wholesale and retail trade	154,544	59.8	28,496	73.5	8,061	72.4	18.4	28.3

Source: OECD (1993a, p. 51).

Note: A Japanese multinational enterprise consists of a Japanese parent (excluding finance, insurance, and real estate industries) and its foreign affiliates. A Japanese parent is a Japanese person who owns or controls 10 percent or more of voting securities of an incorporated foreign business enterprise. Japanese foreign affiliates consist of (1) foreign subsidiaries so controlled by Japanese parents, and (2) foreign business enterprises that are more than 50 percent owned by the majority-owned Japanese foreign subsidiaries ("grandchildren"). The MITI benchmark survey does not provide estimates of the entire universe so that these data are not strictly comparable with those provided by the U.S. Department of Commerce benchmark survey.

Table 1-11. *Estimated Worldwide Sales of Foreign Affiliates and Total Exports, 1982–89, and Average Annual Growth Rates, 1982–84 and 1985–89*

Trillions of dollars

Year	Sales[a]	Exports[b]	Ratio of sales to exports (%)
1982	2.4	1.5	1.6
1983	2.3	1.3	1.7
1984	2.5	1.4	1.7
1985	2.5	1.4	1.8
1986	2.9	1.7	1.7
1987	3.5	2.0	1.7
1988	4.2	2.4	1.8
1989[c]	4.4	2.5	1.8
Average annual growth rates	1982-84	1985-89	
Sales	3	15	
Exports	-2	15	

Source: United Nations (1992, p. 55).

a. Worldwide estimates of sales by foreign affiliates of home-based TNCs were calculated by extrapolating the sales of foreign affiliates of TNCs from the Federal Republic of Germany, Japan, and the United States on the basis of the relative importance of these countries in worldwide FDI outward stock.

b. Worldwide exports have been adjusted to exclude intrafirm trade, estimated by applying the share of intrafirm trade by TNC affiliates in total exports from the United States to worldwide exports.

c. Preliminary estimates extrapolating the sales of foreign affiliates of TNCs from the Federal Republic of Germany and the United States on the same basis as that described in (a).

includes sales to third countries) amounted by $4.4 trillion, which was nearly twice the value of world exports of goods and services (see table 1-11). It appears that *investment as well as trade is an essential route of access to foreign markets.* Global sales of affiliates are highest in the United States (table 1-12), which has the longest history of multinationalization, but they are growing rapidly in Japan, which recorded a surge in outward investment in the second half of the 1980s. There is a marked contrast between inward and outward investment stock and sales in Japan. In 1990 sales of U.S. nonbank affiliates in Japan totaled $62 billion, whereas the sales of majority-owned Japanese affiliates in the United States came to $291 billion.[13]

13. See U.S. Department of Commerce (July 1993, p. 53, table 11.1; and May 1993, p. 99, table 8).

Table 1-12. *Sales of Foreign Affiliates and Total Exports for Selected Home Countries, 1985–89, and Average Annual Growth Rates, 1982–84 and 1985–89*

Country and year	Sales	Ratio of sales to exports (billions of dollars)	Exports[a]
United States			
1985	895	5.6	159
1986	929	5.1	182
1987	1,053	4.8	218
1988	1,195	4.3	278
1989	1,266[b]	4.1	307
Japan[c]			
1985	214	1.8	117
1986	263	1.8	148
1987	379[d]	2.2	172
1988	534[d]	2.6	203
Germany, Federal Republic			
1985	192	1.5	124
1986	237	1.3	176
1987	290	1.3	220
1988	349	1.4	246
1989	372	1.5	251

Average annual growth rates	United States		Japan		Germany, Federal Republic	
	Sales	Exports	Sales	Exports	Sales	Exports
1982–84	–2	–0.3	23	6	3	–5
1985–89	9	18	36[e]	20[e]	18	19

Source: United Nations (1992, p. 56).

a. Adjusted to exclude intrafirm trade, estimated by applying the share of intrafirm trade by TNC affiliates in total exports from the United States to all exports reported here.

b. Not strictly comparable with the previous estimates because of a break in the series resulting from improved coverage of the survey universe in 1989.

c. Fiscal years. Sales for Japan represent only sales by those affiliates that replied to the corresponding question in the survey questionnaire.

d. Including sales by subsidiaries owned by foreign affiliates.

e. 1985–88.

Another indication of the increasing interindustry and intrafirm trade and the growing dominance of multinational enterprises is the growth of trade in components or intermediate inputs. According to a recent study that used input-output tables to distinguish components in the production chain, foreign sourcing has increased markedly since the early 1970s.[14] This trend reflects the growth in foreign investment and international alliances as well as trade liberalization in many countries, and because of it the "national identity" of final products is becoming more and more difficult to judge. By developing an "indicator of international linkage" (a measure of the ratio of foreign to domestic inputs), the study demonstrated that the most globalized industries in the mid-1980s were capital- and technology-intensive operations, and their products represented complex systems: automobiles, aerospace, communications, semiconductor equipment, and computers. Since then the linkage index may have risen because of the increase in foreign direct investment in the second half of the decade, especially in system-product sectors. It is important to note that the trade in intermediate products provides a significant source of the technology that the industrialized countries have used to improve their productivity.[15]

The critical changes in the international economy discussed thus far have been the growing competition in technology-intensive industry, the diffusion of technology via trade, and the rise of the multinational enterprise. Perhaps the most significant change of the 1980s, however, was the surge in foreign direct investment.

The history of foreign direct investment and of today's multinational enterprise goes back to the second half of the nineteenth century.[16] Until the Second World War, such investment was conducted mainly by American and British firms backed by country policies favoring unregulated markets for investment. In contrast, the policies of several countries of continental Europe and Japan leaned more toward protectionism. By the end of the Second World War, U.S. firms accounted for more than half of the accumulated stock of foreign direct investment, and the British share was just over 16 percent. By 1980 the U.S. share had fallen to 40 percent, although the

14. Wyckoff (1993, pp. 8–11).
15. For estimates of the impact of international R&D spillovers via trade, see Coe and Helpman (1993).
16. For historical data and analysis, see Dunning (1993b, esp. chap. 2 and chap. 5).

Table 1-13. *Inward and Outward Average Annual FDI Flows for the Triad, 1980–85, 1986–1990*

Millions of U.S. dollars per year and shares of triad total

Region	1980–85				1986–1990			
	Inward		Outward		Inward		Outward	
	$	%	$	%	$	%	$	%
European Community	10,146	35	14,755	42	36,335	42	56,890	51
United States	18,642	64	13,492	39	48,241	56	18,750	17
Japan	557	2	6,525	19	2,037	2	36,493	33
Triad totals	29,345	100	34,772	100	86,613	100	112,133	100

Source: United Nations (1993a), country tables.

United States was still the dominant foreign investor, while the major European countries and, somewhat later, Japan had increased their share of world direct investment significantly.[17] Thus in the thirty-five years after World War II a growing number of OECD countries became significant players in global investment activities.

These developments reflect competitive pressures on corporations to capture economies of scale and scope, customize products to satisfy changing consumer tastes, and gain access to sophisticated, high-quality networks, both upstream and downstream. The revolution in information and communication technology has been both an enabling factor and a driver, fostering new forms of organization and processes of production. As already mentioned, this and the other forces of globalization—particularly the growing ubiquitousness of the multinational enterprise and trade liberalization—are interdependent and mutually reinforcing. These forces, together with the pressure in multinational firms to reduce the transaction costs associated with different national regulatory regimes, have brought to public attention the need for greater harmonization of domestic policies as part of the international trade agenda. Governments, too, are calling for harmonization, for fear that investment will become "footloose" or "quicksilver" if it wanders from the location of natural resources or from protected local markets.[18] The issue of harmonization is discussed further in chapter 4.

17. Dunning (1993b, p. 17).
18. For a succinct description of the impact of globalization on country policy attitudes, see Dunning (1993a).

After a brief slowdown in the first half of the 1980s, foreign direct investment surged, growing at an average rate of nearly 30 percent per year, which was four times the growth rate of world output and three times that of trade. Eighty percent of the investment was controlled by multinational enterprises from the European Community, the United States, and Japan (see table 1-13). Although the United States was the primary source of investment throughout the 1980s, Japan had become a major supplier for the first time in the postwar years.

Investment in capital- and technology-intensive industries grew faster than in natural-resource and labor-intensive manufacturing. Between 1975 and 1990 the share of these industries in manufacturing's inward stock of foreign direct investment increased from 27 to 40 percent as a result of heavier flows to the OECD countries and the newly industrialized economies of East Asia. The fastest-growing of these industries were in the newly industrialized economies.[19] As already mentioned, such developments would not have been possible without access to knowledge, which, however still varies greatly from industry to industry and country to country. Nevertheless, global R&D seems likely to increase, albeit with some lag following the establishment of a foreign manufacturing base.[20] For multinationals in particular, it is a decided advantage to be able "to detect new overseas technological threats in their infancy and take appropriate defensive measures."[21] Thus effective market access depends not only on trade and investment, but also on the knowledge required to be a strong competitor. As a result, more and more multinational firms are *exploiting* their technology globally and, to a lesser though increasing degree, are gaining *access* to new technology globally through the worldwide diffusion of R&D and through collaboration. The term *technoglobalism* emerged in the 1980s to refer to this activity.[22]

The collaboration that helped strengthen the link between investment and technology flows began in earnest in the 1980s and took the

19. United Nations (1993b, pp. 70–74). For U.S. data showing the growth of inward and outward foreign direct investment stock in research-intensive manufacturing, see p. 74.

20. For a recent review of existing literature on the subject of R&D globalization, see Freeman and Hagedoorn (1992).

21. Scherer (1992, p. 184).

22. For a critical review of its precise meaning, see Archibugi and Michie (1992–93). The term is widely used in Japan, where it denotes a policy concept involving strategic alliances. See Japan Economic Institute Report (1993, pp. 18–19).

form of joint agreements or, as they are sometimes termed, international strategic alliances, among firms in the major industrialized countries. Although such agreements have long been used to facilitate foreign direct investment, little information is available on the precise arrangements they entail. There is evidence, however, to suggest that over the 1980s these alliances increased noticeably in three areas: biotechnology, information technology, and new materials. Between 1991 and 1992 their number in the pharmaceutical and biotechnology industries rose from fifty-eight to ninety.[23] The increase in transnational R&D agreements was most rapid, no doubt because of escalating R&D costs and the need to monitor a growing spectrum of technologies.[24] Moreover, until the late 1980s antitrust laws discouraged American firms in the same line of business from entering R&D and production alliances, and therefore they began to link up with foreign ones. Another reason for such alliances is that they gave multinational enterprises access to markets and low-cost capital. In general, they offer enterprises a more flexible and less costly way of achieving a range of objectives than does a merger or acquisition. Furthermore, like traditional foreign direct investment, the international strategic alliance offers a means of responding to protectionist pressure.[25] This international spillover of domestic industrial policy is discussed in chapter 2.

Foreign investment flows slowed down in the early 1990s, largely because of slower growth in the advanced countries, but there are signs that it is now picking up. (Even if flows subside for a period, the size of the underlying stock, estimated at nearly $2 trillion in 1991, ensures that multinational enterprises will continue to grow because they are investing their retained earnings.) However, the bulge of the 1980s is not likely to be repeated because it was in part the result of special factors, including trade policy developments in both the E.U. and the United States.

One of the striking features of the 1980s was the enormous increase in Japanese investment outflow, from $6½ billion in 1980–85 to $36.5 billion in 1986–90 (table 1-13). This outflow has been attributed to several factors, including the marked increase in the

23. U.S. Congress (1993, p. 118).
24. See Hagedoorn (1990, pp. 17–30).
25. See Mowery (1991, pp. 29–62).

Table 1-14. Inward and Outward Stocks of FDI by Regions and Countries, 1980, 1985, 1990
Billions of dollars and world shares

Country/region	1990 Inward $	%	1990 Outward $	%	1985 Inward $	%	1985 Outward $	%	1980 Inward $	%	1980 Outward $	%
World	1,638.9	100.0	1,644.0	100.0	727.1	100.0	678.2	100.0	505.3	100.0	516.9	100.0
Developed economies	1,328.9	81.1	1,593.0	96.9	544.5	74.9	656.3	96.8	394.1	78.0	503.6	97.4
Triad	1,053.2	64.3	1,342.7	81.7	413.9	56.9	563.1	83.0	273.2	54.1	440.0	85.1
European Community	646.6	39.5	714.8	43.5	224.6	30.9	268.1	39.5	186.9	37.0	200.2	38.7
France	71.8	4.4	114.8	7.0	31.9	4.4	31.5	4.6	21.1	4.2	20.8	4.0
Germany	132.5	8.1	155.1	9.4	49.5	6.8	59.9	8.8	47.9	9.5	43.1	8.3
United Kingdom	205.6	12.5	244.8	14.9	62.6	8.6	101.2	14.9	63.0	12.5	79.2	15.3
United States	396.7	24.2	426.5	25.9	184.6	25.4	251.0	37.0	83.0	16.4	220.2	42.6
Japan	9.9	0.6	201.4	12.2	4.7	0.6	44.0	6.5	3.3	0.7	19.6	3.8
Triad/world	64.3		81.7		56.9		83.0		54.1		85.1	

Source: Rutter (1992, appendixes 3 and 8).

Japanese current account surplus over the 1980s, which turned Japan into a major capital exporter.[26] But this cannot alone explain why the form of export was foreign direct investment rather than portfolio investment. Other factors at work were U.S. and European trade policies, Japan's relaxation of controls on capital exports, changes in the relative cost of capital in Japan and other countries, and the sharp drop in the value of the dollar against the yen after the 1985 Plaza Agreement. Thus, although Japan's current account surplus cannot be *directly* linked to the behavior of Japanese multinational enterprises in the 1980s, the *indirect* effects—especially the fear of trade disagreements and the marked rise in the yen—created economic incentive and a political impetus, in Japan and abroad, to encourage investment rather than to rely on exports alone as a means of penetrating foreign markets.

Ironically, this investment outflow has merely created new sources of friction, most apparent in the United States in the 1980s. The reaction to Japanese multinational enterprises is reminiscent of the complaints in the 1960s of the "economic invasion" of Europe, which some predicted would make it a subsidiary of the United States.[27] Whereas that crisis was eventually defused by significant European investment in America, however, the rapid outflow from Japan occurred just when the level of foreign multinational presence in Japan was at an all-time low (see table 1-14). Since effective market access depends on both trade and investment, this situation created further high-tech friction in the 1980s.

As this chapter has shown, these conflicts were the eventual outcome of the decline of American hegemony and the rise of the powerful forces of globalization, which both sped that decline and tightened the trade, investment, and technology links among the industrialized countries and thereby made possible the *technoglobalism* that has come to characterize the world economy in recent years. The division of labor among the advanced countries is determined in large part by the ability of their multinational enterprises to create new ideas and products. This ability, in turn, depends on the benefits flowing from global markets. Chapter 2 reviews the national policies designed to help high-tech industries become more innovative and discusses the emergence of *technonationalism*.

26. See Graham and Krugman (1989).
27. Servan-Schreiber (1968, p. 23).

Chapter 2

National Innovation Systems, Industrial Policies, and the Rise of Technonationalism

A COMPLEX set of institutions and policies has grown up around high-tech industries in various countries. This chapter lays out their most salient differences. It also considers the kinds of "market failures" associated with technical progress that provide an economic rationale for significant government involvement in sectors where technical advance is important. In addition, attention is given to some elements of strategic trade theory which suggests a "beggar thy neighbor" flavor to technology policies. The heart of the chapter is concerned with the concept of "national innovation systems." This concept is used to explore how and why the systems have evolved differently in the major industrial nations. The chapter closes with a discussion of the national policies of the 1980s. The central theme is that the current international conflict is largely a result of the attempt of governments to impose national technology policies on a world in which business and technology are increasingly transnational.

Technical Advance and "Market Failure"

Economists studying technical advance have long recognized a bestiary of "market failures."[1] High-technology industries tend to have high up-front R&D costs and in many cases require large physical investments before they can produce or employ a new product or process, even on a small scale. Thus these industries tend to have

---

1. See, for example, Stoneman (1987); and Nelson (1990, pp. 193–214).

nonconvexities. Under these circumstances, competition—in the sense of several companies designing and producing a product—may be associated with higher-than-needed total R&D costs. Experience indicates, however, that firms without strong technological rivals tend to rest on their laurels.

A firm that performs R&D usually is unable to keep the technology behind its new products and processes completely privy, and sooner or later its competitors are going to be able to draw significantly from the new technology it has created to fashion their own substitutes. Thus R&D can have substantial externalities or spillovers. If a firm is unable to appropriate fully the returns to its investments, it will tend to underinvest in that activity, from a social point of view. Note, too, that the creation of a new product or process is almost always associated with the creation of new knowledge or understanding—this is what makes imitation possible—and such new knowledge has public good in the sense that it costs less to disseminate the knowledge to a number of parties than to have each of the parties create or discover that knowledge on its own. Thus if the inventor or discoverer were to restrict access to technological knowledge and its use, which it would have to do to reap the full returns from its investments, other sorts of inefficiency problems might arise. For one thing, a company that is denied access will operate with inferior technology. And although it could spend its own money on R&D, it might come up with a technology that is no better than the technology it was denied.

Economic theory would hold that if license markets were perfect, a company with a fully effective blocking patent on a technology it created would be able to strike deals with its competitors, giving them access in return for royalty payments. In fact, the licensing and cross-licensing of technology is a widespread practice in many industries. However, the market for technology licenses has been shown to be highly imperfect. Most of the licensing between firms in the same line of business goes on in one of two contexts. In many cases, the firms have staked out different markets, for example, through regional market splitting.[2] Considerable cross-licensing also occurs where firms have agreed not to enforce their patents on each other.

Cross-licensing, or mutual restraint in enforcing patents, is widespread in industries whose product and process technologies consti-

---

2. Caves, Crookell, and Killing (1983, pp. 249–67).

tute complex systems. In such industries technical advance generally consists of changing one or a few parts of the system, but not the whole, and the patents on these different parts of the system are invariably owned by different firms. If the firms try to enforce their patents on each other, no one is able to operate a "best-practice" system. Indeed, if the patent rights are strongly enforced, firms may even be prohibited from implementing their own inventions because they cannot do so without infringing on someone else's property rights. For this reason, and others, except in a small number of industries, few firms use patent protection as the principal means of capturing the return from their innovation. There are exceptions. In particular in pharmaceuticals and in fine chemicals, companies rely heavily on patent protection to enable them to profit from their R&D. But in semiconductors, computers, telecommunications, and aircraft, companies reap returns mainly by achieving a head start on their rivals, which they then exploit by seizing the market and moving rapidly down the learning curve. They fully expect their rivals to pick up and use their inventions, but with a lag.[3]

In earlier years, the lag was often considerable, but, in recent years speedy imitation is harder to hold off, and even newcomers are among the speedy imitators. On the other hand, as also mentioned, some of the gentlemen's agreements not to enforce patents have begun to break down. American companies, in particular, have been advocating stronger enforcement of intellectual property rights on firms based in other countries. As those foreign firms themselves begin work at the frontiers of systems technologies, which many are already doing, efforts to enforce intellectual property rights will become a two-edged sword.

Because of these problems, many economists are backing away from the idea that intellectual property rights should be enforced strongly to induce industrial innovation and are arguing that government support of R&D is the way to deal with these externalities. This view, however, runs counter to the view expressed by other economists that government-supported R&D programs are inevitably inefficient and devised simply to give a nation's companies an unfair advantage over their rivals in other countries. Such subsidies may indeed provide those national firms with a significant advantage and

3. Levin and others (1987, pp. 783–820).

may enable industry leaders to maintain their market position, for although it is impossible to keep nationally developed technologies within national borders, diffusion takes time.

This latter notion falls under the heading of "strategic trade theory."[4] Strategic trade theory is a collection of ideas introduced over the past decade that has to do with the features of international competition in industries where technical advance is the principal means of competition. One of these ideas is that if an industry has large up-front R&D and other investment costs, the world market may be able to sustain only a small number of firms. Furthermore, in that oligopolistic market structure, the firms in the industry may be able to earn returns that are significantly higher than those earned in more competitive industries and at the same time pay their work force higher wages, without inducing entry. Therefore, it is argued, market failure may justify government R&D support or protection of the home market as an implicit subsidy. Since other countries also see these possibilities, a country that seizes them first (and forecloses the market for firms in other countries) or pursues them most aggressively and sustainedly (and thus forces firms in other countries out of the business) can reap significant national returns.

A related argument has been put forth to explain the stagnation in real wages in the American economy over the past twenty years. The proposition is that increased foreign competition, a flood of imports, and a reduction of export markets have led to the "deindustrialization" of the United States. Foreign competition has cost the country its high-wage industrial jobs. A counterargument is that the fraction of the work force employed in manufacturing has declined because productivity in manufacturing has grown at a much higher rate than productivity in other parts of the economy, particularly in services. While the prices of manufactured products have fallen in relation to the prices of services, in high-income countries, the demand for manufactured goods is price inelastic.[5] Thus, although consumers are buying more manufactured goods, the increase is not sufficient to offset the decline in the labor required to produce a given quantity of goods. Various studies have purported to show that the increase in imports as a fraction of total consumption of manufactured goods in

4. For a discussion of strategic trade theory, see Krugman (1987).
5. Clarida and Hickok (1993, pp. 173–92).

the United States accounts for only a small fraction of the decline in employment in manufacturing. Also, as discussed in chapter 1, in recent years the United States has done quite well in exports of manufactured goods, particularly of the high-tech variety.[6]

The proponents of the deindustrialization argument respond that average wages in manufacturing, especially in the high-tech industries, continue to be significantly higher than average wages in the services. In their view, real income in the United States would be larger if less of the manufacturing market were cut away by imports and if American firms had greater access to closed foreign markets, particularly those of Japan. Had the demand for labor by American manufacturing companies been greater, they claim, manufacturing wages would not have stagnated to the extent now seen.[7]

The debate concerning deindustrialization and its causes has thus far been of a general nature, and has only touched on the high-tech aspects of the issue, although some observers have pointed out that high-tech industry is an important source of high-paying jobs and that the United States needs to preserve them. These industries, it is also argued, are strategic in another sense. They yield externalities that are by and large localized geographically. Furthermore, their products are used mainly by other firms and they generate downstream externalities. Thus the benefits of the new technologies introduced by the producers of equipment for manufacturing semiconductors flow to a considerable degree to the companies that first buy and use the new equipment. New improved semiconductors in turn yield benefits to the companies that buy them and employ them in their products, for example, computers and telecommunications equipment. To the extent that interfirm relations upstream and downstream are intranational, the benefit of supporting national upstream high-tech firms spills over to national firms downstream.[8]

There is probably something to all of these arguments, although perhaps less than their strongest proponents claim. One of the problems is that the increasing competition in high-tech industries is undercutting their ability to earn significantly higher than competitive returns and pay higher than competitive wages. Another is that, with the globalization of industry, geographical proximity and intra-

6. See National Science Board (1993, appendix table 6-4, pp. 440–46).
7. For a balanced discussion, see Levy and Murnane (1992, pp. 1333–81).
8. Tyson (1992).

national interfirm linkages have begun losing some of their force. And, as discussed in the next section, government policies designed to capture the benefits or spillovers may actually accelerate globalization or diffusion.

Traditional economic theory can provide some insight into the issues being debated. It is useful, for example, to see some government policies as stepping in "where markets work poorly" and others as helping a high-wage national industry become an effective competitor or helping to internalize externalities. From this perspective, however, little is seen of the complex institutional structures that have grown up around high-tech industries or the strong connections between some of these industries and certain governmental objectives—or the striking differences in these structures and connections across industries. A recent body of empirical research on national innovation systems and their evolution has addressed just these matters.[9]

National Innovation Systems

The modern science-based industry is a relatively recent development. One of its distinctive features is the industrial research and development laboratory, which is owned by a particular firm, staffed by university-trained scientists and engineers, and dedicated to advancing the mother firm's product and process technologies. Another important feature is the presence of scientific and technical societies, whose members include the research and development scientists and engineers employed by business firms, university researchers, and in many cases, scientists and engineers working in government laboratories or agencies. These societies hold regular meetings, publish journals, and in general serve to keep their professional members informed about the scientific and technical news in their fields. The presence and nature of these scientific societies reflects the fact that almost all high-tech industries have given rise to various fields of academic research, such as electrical engineering, material science, computer science, and oncology. These have become established disciplines in universities, and the research emanating from them helps industrial R&D come up with new products and processes.

9. Much of the analysis that follows is drawn from Nelson (1993).

A century or so ago, technical progress was achieved mainly through the efforts of individual inventors, or small groups of them, who gained their skills by and large through practical experience. Very few of these inventors had university training in a field of science or technology; indeed, what universities taught was generally of little use to industrial inventing. Although a variety of journals for mechanics or inventors spread the news, nothing like the present-day elaborate network of scientific and technical societies existed. Only a small amount of scientific research went on in universities, and even that had little relevance to practical problem solving.

Since then, the system of technical innovation has changed radically, owing to the modern industrial research and development laboratory, the professionalization of inventing, and the research university, all of which evolved in tandem. Also, from the beginning national governments took a strong interest in new technologies and industries. Well before World War I governments were aware of the importance to national security of radio and aircraft technologies, for example. The new chemical industries were the developers of high explosives, and for nations like Germany that feared being cut off from the rest of the world in any war, they were an invaluable source of synthetic substitutes. In virtually all of the major industrial nations, strong ties grew up between the new high-tech firms and government agencies concerned with telecommunications, air transport, health, and defense.

World War II was a watershed in the history of government policies concerned with the development of science and technology. Until then such policies had been limited in their spending and scope. The central importance of science and technology to military strength was made dramatically visible in World War II. After the war, the governments of industrial nations for the first time took on prime responsibility for the funding of university research, generally at levels far above those of the prewar period. In most countries the government funding came from two sources: agencies expressly set up to support university research across a broad front (such as the National Science Foundation in the United States), and established agencies that funded university research in fields associated with their basic mission, by and large defense, atomic energy, or health. Also, the number and size of government laboratories, particularly in these three fields, expanded greatly.

Countries that had a sizable defense procurement program or a space program began pouring funds into R&D in industries associated with the procurement of systems. In the 1960s government-financed R&D in these areas accounted for more than half of total industrial R&D in the United States. France and the United Kingdom followed a similar path. Contrary to popular belief, however, this funding of industrial R&D was restricted almost entirely to government programs in defense and space (the Concorde and Airbus are exceptions) and thus to industries that produce systems for defense and space.

As pointed out in chapter 1, the postwar era also saw a vast increase in private spending on industrial R&D, first in the United States and later in Europe and Japan. Except in countries with large defense programs, private spending has accounted for by far the lion's share of the growth of industrial R&D as a fraction of GNP. And with the end of the cold war, the United States, France, and Britain are likely to make deep cuts in government funding of industrial R&D.

From the foregoing it appears that the contemporary innovation systems of the major industrial nations have a great deal in common. This is not so surprising since the same forces have shaped their systems. Moreover, nations tend to look to each other for policy and design guidance. In the early years of the twentieth century many nations, including the United States, looked to Germany as a model of how a university research system should be organized. From the end of World War II to 1980, most nations looked to the United States as a general model. Since the mid-1980s the Europeans, and to a considerable extent the Americans, have looked to Japan, while Japan has begun to emulate some aspects of American and European systems. Despite the resulting similarities, national innovation systems still differ in many respects, reflecting differences in history, the relative importance of national security and other objectives in guiding a nation's policy, and other variables. The principal differences between the systems of the United States, Japan, and some parts of Europe are briefly discussed in the remainder of this section.

The United States

The high-technology industries of the United States grew up in a protected setting. The industries producing chemical products and electrical equipment were, from their beginnings, shielded from European competition by tariffs and the strong preference of customers to "buy American."[10] This was also the case with the American aircraft and aircraft engine industries. With the exception of organic chemical products, where Germany had a significant technological lead, the protection probably was not needed. In fact, American firms in the electrical equipment industry quickly became major exporters. But the protection was there. Another important point to note is that in the period after World War II the American semiconductor and computer industries grew up by producing mainly for the American military, whose market was reserved primarily for American firms.

Thus although Americans often think of themselves as being staunch and steady supporters of free and open trade, that was not the American creed or policy before Bretton Woods and GATT. And although today Americans take umbrage at the policies of other countries that shelter government procurement, over the postwar era the United States has preserved for its firms the lion's share of what has been the world's largest procurement market.

Before World War II the U.S. government played a major role in supporting and guiding technical advance in only a few areas. One of these was agriculture. Indeed, in the years just before World War II the federal government spent more on agricultural research than it did on research oriented toward national security.

Another exception was aeronautics. The U.S. experience during World War I had demonstrated the military importance of aircraft, and after the war the government established the National Advisory Commission on Aeronautics and gave it a small budget to support the development of both civil and military aviation in the United States. During the 1920s the federal government stepped in to prevent radio technology, which had proved so important during World War I, from falling into foreign (British) hands and played an active role in establishing an American-owned company—RCA—as the national champion in the development of radio. Also just before World War II, the armed forces supported university research dedicated to developing faster "computers." By and large, however, the government provided only a small amount of direct support for the development of industrial technology.

10. The discussion of the U.S. system is drawn largely from Mowery and Rosenberg (1993, pp. 29–75).

After World War II the federal government took on responsibility for funding university research across the board. As a result, by the 1960s the American university research system was generally considered preeminent. A large fraction of this funding flowed into applied fields, particularly those related to health and to defense technologies. American research in biology and in fields such as computer and materials science and electrical engineering became especially strong. In fields relating to defense and space, government funding of industrial R&D soon came to outstrip private funding. Although there is no evidence to indicate that support from the Department of Defense and the National Aeronautics and Space Administration was deliberately used to help American firms become dominant in civilian markets for semiconductors, computers, and commercial aircraft, this was certainly one of the consequences of these programs.

Up until 1970 or so, the military market was by far the largest and most demanding market for these products. After that, the civilian market for computers, semiconductors, and aircraft overtook the military market, and began attracting large-scale private R&D funding. Because the technological demands of the civilian markets tended to be different from those of military procurement, the civil R&D and production industry gradually separated itself from the military. As a result, spillover effects grew less and less important.

During the 1980s Japan gained enormous strength in technological fields that used to be dominated by the United States. Spurred by a growing concern about this turn of events, the United States began to experiment with a number of programs expressly designed to support the competitive prowess of U.S. industry in those fields. The government was able to support the Microelectronics and Computer Technology Corporation, by amending U.S. antitrust law to make American companies less fearful about establishing cooperative research organizations. Other policies involved significant infusions of public money, in the form of public-private research associations such as Sematech. The Reagan and Bush administrations, however, were reluctant to push very far in these directions. On the other hand, the rhetoric under the Clinton administration is much more favorable to these kinds of developments.

What is there to say, then, about American policy aimed at supporting technical advance in industry? First of all, the situation is far more complex than many believe. The government is involved and channels funds in technological developments in certain fields, but its involvement is very uneven across fields. However, to date, with the exception of national security and closely related fields, U.S. policy has not provided for the heavy subsidization of R&D that takes place in industry. By and large, U.S. technology policy has, in fact, had no overall or comprehensive strategic intent: the policy has been implicit rather than explicit.

For the purposes of this discussion, three aspects of the current American innovation system merit attention. The first is the central role universities play both in basic research and in research in the applied sciences and engineering disciplines. The Japanese do not yet have anything that approaches the American university research system. They do much less basic research than the Americans, and a larger fraction of it goes on in government laboratories or in the laboratories of corporations. Germany used to have an outstanding university research system, but it has fallen into decline since World War II. As a result, a significant share of German research not done in corporations takes place in special-purpose public laboratories rather than in universities. In addition, a significantly larger fraction of scientists and engineers in the United States, including foreign students, obtain their advanced training in universities than do their counterparts in Japan or Germany, where training takes place primarily within the company or in a research institute. During the 1980s, however, university research in the United States began receiving considerable support from firms, including foreign firms.

A second notable feature of the American innovation system is an outgrowth of the country's long-standing respect for antitrust laws and its strong venture capital market. Because of antitrust concerns, the United States did not develop the tightly knit oligopolistic structures of coordination typical of high-tech industry in Germany and elsewhere in Europe, at least in the period before World War II (although, as mentioned earlier, cross-licensing of technology was common). Nor did it permit structures like Japan's zaibatsu and keiretsu to develop. Furthermore, unlike Europe and Japan, it allowed far more new firms to enter into high-technology areas. In many cases, the new firms were started by American academics or drew significantly on American academic research. Small firms starting up in high-tech sectors also received considerable impetus from the high levels of labor mobility both from universities and between firms.

The third prominent characteristic of the American innovation system is that relations between the government and industry are often of an adversarial nature. Furthermore, industry and a large percentage of the American electorate are strongly resistant to having the government involved in decisions that can be seen as pushing winners. Although the government has been heavily involved in the U.S. defense industries and a few other (generally related) cases, there is nothing in the United States like the tradition of government tutorage and protection that one sees in Japan and, earlier at least, in Germany.

All three of these characteristics have imbued the American system with a high degree of structural openness, which contrasts sharply with Japan's closed structure.

Japan

In part because of Japan's economic and technological history, Japanese attitudes toward the appropriate role of the government in the economy differ considerably from those prevalent in the United States.[11] Some of these attitudes date back to the Meiji restoration of 1868, when central power reverted from military families to the emperor. The emperor's supporters argued that a strong central government was needed to enable Japan to transform its economy and gain mastery of technology along Western lines so that it could overcome its military inferiority and stand up to Western pressures. That continued to be Japan's goal through World War II. And that is why in those early days most of Japan's large firms were directly involved either in military production (as in ship building) or in the production of materials used in military production (such as steel).

Although the government played a leading role as entrepreneur, coordinator, and financier of new firms bringing in Western technology, by the early twentieth century a strong entrepreneurial class had grown up in Japan, and many new firms and industries were being created in response to market-driven forces. In the years just before World War I and throughout much of the interwar period, most of the new Japanese firms in fields such as electrical equipment and automobile production were either partners or subsidiaries of Western

11. The following discussion is drawn largely from Odagiri and Goto (1993, pp. 76–114).

firms. During the 1930s, however, the Japanese military took strong measures to reduce Japanese dependency on Western skills in industries deemed vital to the military. Electrical equipment suppliers were pulled away from their Western partners, the market for automobiles was gradually closed to Western exporters, and producers were encouraged to cut loose their Western ties. Japan also developed its own aircraft industry.

The post–World War II industrial structure clearly has its roots in the industries built during the interwar period. For the first few years after the war, Japan was extremely short on foreign exchange. Reindustrialization was slow until the advent of the Korean War, whereupon the United States decided to use Japanese industry as a procurement base. When the Korean War ended, much of Japanese industry was back on its feet, although it once again had to be weaned from military markets. It is important to understand that a good share of Japanese industry that has been so successful competing in civilian markets since that time arose in an environment where national security interests were central.

Although American military procurement during the Korean War temporarily relieved Japan's foreign exchange constraints, these constraints reappeared at the end of the war. In response, the Japanese government decided first to provide strong incentives, including moral incentives, to encourage Japanese industry to export; and second to keep foreign exchange under tight governmental control. The government was able to oversee the allocation of investment in Japanese industries and particular firms, through the control of licenses necessary for importing capital equipment and materials that Japanese industry was not yet able to produce for itself. Over this same period, there were strong restrictions on imports of commodities that the government thought Japan could produce for itself, or that the government wanted Japanese industry to begin producing. And whereas American companies had been able to use foreign subsidiaries to leap over the protective walls erected in Europe, in Japan this was impossible. Thus the firms in the Japanese electrical equipment, automobile, and other heavy industries that had loosened their Western connections before World War II were able to grow up again as purely Japanese national firms.

Even before the Meiji restoration, education was widespread in Japan and literacy high by European standards. By World War II Japan had therefore been able to educate a large number of world-class engineers. In the period after World War II Japan continued to push hard on the education front. Although there is much innuendo about the quality of Japanese higher education in science and engineering, the extreme complaints are certainly exaggerated. By the mid-1960s Japanese industry was able to staff itself with sufficient numbers of qualified engineers to begin its strong run on the American techno-logical lead in automobiles, and particularly electronics. Although Japanese companies apparently provide a larger share of an engineer's training in their own facilities than is the case in the United States, the mix of university and company training in Japan seems to work quite well. By the mid-1980s the ratio of scientists and engineers to the total work force in Japan was close to levels in the United States.

There is no question that the Ministry of Finance, the Ministry of International Trade and Industry (MITI), and the Japanese public sector telephone company, NTT, together played a powerful role in molding the evolution of Japanese manufacturing industry during the 1960s and into the 1970s. The control of foreign exchange and the ability to block both imports and direct foreign investment were particularly effective instruments during the early part of this period. Analysts are divided on the importance of MITI's "visions" and guidance during this period, but when backed by control over the allocation of resources, the ministry undoubtedly had considerable influence. There is also some difference of opinion regarding the importance of various cooperative programs for industrial research orchestrated and partly funded through MITI and NTT. Certainly in the early parts of this era these programs clearly helped Japanese industry bring its companies up to world standards.

By the late 1960s, however, the government had begun to lose some of its leverage. Because Japan had joined GATT and was easing up on foreign exchange constraints, the government lost its ability to control access to a valuable scarce resource. At the same time, Japan-ese industry was rapidly expanding and producing items that earlier could only be obtained through imports. Then during the 1970s and 1980s the previously closed Japanese financial market became more open. As their profits swelled, companies had less need for bank finance. This, in turn, meant the government had less control over the allocation of finance. By the early 1980s Japanese technology was up to world-class levels in many areas. The famous cooperative research programs joined by various industries and sponsored by NTT and

MITI now began to aim for technological supremacy, not just parity. Many of Japan's industrialists argued that cooperative research would not be a powerful enough instrument for this new purpose.

From all accounts of the Japanese economy during the 1980s, government intervention had clearly declined from its earlier levels, although inherited structural barriers to entry by either imports or investment still had an effect on technology policy. Thus Americans and Europeans no longer complained that the Japanese government was doing something different and unfair, but that the complex Japanese way of doing business was strongly biased against foreign products and firms. This complaint soon blossomed into the so-called structural impediments negotiations, discussed in chapter 3.

In some cases, the impediment consisted of a cozy relationship between a Japanese government agency and a group of Japanese firms. More often, entry was difficult to gain because of the complex web of interaction and mutual assistance among Japanese firms structured under the keiretsu system and supported by banks with a direct interest in the collections of firms. All the while, government organizations like MITI were still hovering in the background.

Europe

Since World War II the United States has been the world's preeminent technological power, with Japan close behind since the late 1970s and even in the lead in some areas in recent years. For much of this time Western Europe has been in the rear. Clearly bothered by their position, the nations of Europe have mounted a series of programs designed to bring them closer to parity with the United States. Japan, meanwhile, has continued to be a source of concern and a spur to action. Yet in the view of Europeans, nothing has worked. Their frustration about being behind in high technology was one of the powerful forces behind the moves toward closer economic integration. Since the early 1980s, Pan-European technology programs have proliferated. Some of these are discussed later in the chapter.

It appears, however, that the cultural, historical, and institutional differences among the major European nations will severely limit the breadth and depth of these common programs and that the nations will to a large extent continue to go their own way. Therefore it is important to be aware of some of the key elements of the national innovation systems of the major European economies.

GREAT BRITAIN. Great Britain was the world's technological as well as economic leader for most of the nineteenth century.[12] The eclipse of Britain by Germany and the United States has therefore attracted a great deal of scholarly attention. Some say that it fell so far behind Germany and the United States in developing new chemical products and electrical equipment industries toward the end of the nineteenth century because the owners of British firms neglected to make the needed investments. A strong case can also be made that Britain initially lacked the institutions that were needed to capitalize on new science-based technologies and only built them up slowly.

It has also been suggested that British universities failed to develop the kind of university training programs that grew up in these other countries. Thus British firms in the new organic chemical products industry did not have the supply of native-born, university-trained chemists that German, and later American, firms had and had to rely to a large extent on German chemists. Certainly, the top British scientists were as good as those anywhere and received their fair share of Nobel prizes. Britain could also boast of having developed radar during World War II and of achieving other important advances, notably in chemical and electrical products. Compared with their counterparts in the United States and Germany, however, the British scientific and technical work force lacked depth and breadth, and few British companies made the large investments in technology that American and German firms did. The problem, some say, is that the universities made few trained scientists and engineers available. Others argue that the fault lay with British companies, which, with few exceptions, did not show much interest in having them.

In Great Britain, as in the United States, World War II brought dramatic changes in the system of doing and supporting science and technology. As in the United States, there was a significant increase in government funding of academic research and military R&D. Public funds flowed into the development of electronics, nuclear power, and, in the early postwar days, into the development of civilian aircraft. By the early 1960s, however, it was evident that the British electronics industry was far behind the American. Despite initial significant

12. This discussion is based largely on Walker (1993, pp. 158–91).

government funding, the British civil aircraft industry never achieved commercial viability and gradually fell into decline, except in the field of aircraft engines.

Since the end of World War II, technology policy has been one of the areas of dispute between the Conservative and Labor parties. In the view of the Conservative party as a whole, government leadership and direct involvement in civilian manufacturing industry are a mistake. In contrast, from the time of its first postwar administration, the Labor party has advocated aggressive technology and industrial policies. The Conservative regimes of the 1980s and early 1990s have pulled away from the active policies put in place earlier by Labor governments, and, with the end of the cold war, reduced their support of military R&D. Although the era of Conservative rule may be coming to a close, it is highly unlikely that Britain will resume active technology policies in the near future.

FRANCE. In the early twentieth century French industry lagged behind Germany and the United States and even Britain in developing high-technology industries.[13] Like Britain, France has always had a small cadre of world-class scientists and engineers, but its weakness has been in the breadth and depth of the science and technology being developed.

Whereas in Great Britain, Germany, and the United States modern scientific research grew up in the universities, in France institutions of higher education specialized in training, while research came to be located in separate institutions (although university facility members in many cases were affiliated with those institutions). Furthermore, the universities were oriented to train people for public service rather than for industry. Although this was also the case in Germany in the early nineteenth century, by the late nineteenth century German universities and technical schools had reoriented themselves to the needs of industries. In France this did not happen, and apparently it has not happened yet.

In France, as in Britain, it may be that universities did not train scientists and engineers to go out into industry because industry was not interested in hiring them.

Following the trauma of defeat and occupation during World War II, a new generation of highly educated individuals came to power

---

13. This discussion is based largely on Chesnais (1993, pp. 192–229).

who were dedicated to modernizing the French economy. Unlike the United States and Great Britain, France had no tradition of ideological or pragmatic resistance to government intervention in the economy. On the contrary, such intervention was deemed fit and proper, perhaps even necessary, a view that goes back to the seventeenth century and the days of Colbert. In the early postwar era, French bureaucrats, like the Japanese, had the instruments to allocate resources across a broad front. They could control the allocation of foreign exchange and access to the internal banking system, and thus had considerable leverage over investment. Once foreign exchange was in greater supply and firms had more access to capital, and import competition increased, the government no longer had broad control over allocation. The situation was not unlike that in Japan a decade later. However, the French government retained a considerable amount of specific control over specific sectors through its defense programs and through its ownership of the electric power, and telecommunication systems. In addition, a nontrivial fraction of the large firms in the chemical products, automobile, and steel industries had been nationalized after the war.

A primary goal of the civil servant modernizers is to bring France to the forefront of advanced technologies, particularly in the aircraft, and electronics fields. Under French policy, particular firms have been given a mandate and the resources to advance particular technologies, with a view to developing "national champions." In contrast, Japanese policy, although it offered protection from foreign competition, in general encouraged internal competition.

Until recently France's technology and industrial policies were strongly influenced by its desire to be an independent and strong military power. The support of civil aviation, from the early postwar work on commercial jet aircraft to the development of the SST and the Airbus, has been part and parcel of a policy geared toward sustaining France's capability to design and produce military aircraft. In the 1960s, when the United States refused to allow the sale of an IBM computer to the French atomic authority, French policymakers turned their attention to establishing a domestic computer and semiconductor industry. Although the military connection became attenuated after the mid-1970s, French technology policy still shows the signs of an interest in "dual-use" technologies, as well as a penchant for supporting national champions.

The results of these various efforts have been very uneven. On one hand, French companies are still not competitive with American or Japanese firms in computers or semiconductors. On the other hand, French nuclear reactors are of superior quality, although, as luck would have it, the world market for nuclear reactors has dried up in the past twenty years. The supersonic transport was a technological triumph, but it continues to be extremely expensive to operate and a chronic drain on the French treasury. Airbus may be more of an economic success.

France's productivity and per capita income have grown quite rapidly over the past thirty years, with the result that the country now ranks with Germany as a European economic success story. Some would argue, however, that the increase in productivity and living standards has had little to do with the large-scale investments in military technology and other high-tech policies. In the past decade, France has been retreating from these policies and has privatized a number of long-standing national companies. And in programs such as Airbus ESPRIT and Eureka, the French have been leaning toward a Pan-European technology policy.

GERMANY. Industrial development in Germany was delayed by the wars of the eighteenth and early nineteenth centuries and by political fragmentation.[14] It only began in earnest with the creation of the Zollverein and subsequent political unification. After unification, however, German industrialization proceeded at a rapid rate, and by the beginning of the twentieth century German industry clearly had surpassed the British in the high-technology fields of the new era, chemical products and electrical equipment.

Even earlier, by 1870 or so, German universities had become widely regarded as the world's leaders in research and teaching in the natural sciences. Although originally established to train civil servants, the universities broadened their goals once the new chemistry- and physics-based industries came into existence. The German university system gave German industry a strong advantage over its competitors in other countries in terms of access to university-trained scientists. Engineering training in Germany was soon turned over to the Technische Hochschulen. German firms in the chemical industry pioneered the establishment of industrial research laboratories staffed

14. This discussion is based largely on Keck (1993, pp. 115–57).

by university-trained scientists. In the electrical equipment industry, German firms shared with the Americans leadership in industrial R&D.

Early on, Germany had also developed a first-rate system of vocational and technical education for students at the secondary school level. Its strong support of science education at all levels was one of the keys to the successful development of German industry. In addition, Germany's military buildup for World War I and World War II contributed to the development of heavy industry: steel, ship building, mechanical engineering, and chemical and electrical products. In this respect, Germany's experience was similar to that of Japan.

Germany's rapid economic recovery in the 1950s after heavy wartime destruction and the postwar division of the country was hailed as an "economic miracle." Most of the strong industries that emerged at this time had been strong and competitive before World War II. And although some aspects of the prewar German system were preserved, many others changed dramatically. For one thing, close contact between German universities and German industry was now discouraged. In time, German universities were replaced by American universities as the leaders in research and graduate education in the natural sciences. As noted earlier, one source of American postwar strength in high-technology industries was the close connection between universities and industry. Many Germans attribute the country's postwar weakness in these industries to the lack of such interactions.

Another major change was the sharp departure from the old notion that national security interests warranted government intervention in the shaping of German industrial development. The German reaction in this regard appears to have been much stronger than that of Japan. Shortly after the war, German political leaders began to articulate an American-like free-enterprise philosophy. With its military programs greatly limited after the war, and even up to the present, Germany never mounted anything like the large-scale support of industrial R&D in electronics and aircraft that was amassed in the United States, Britain, and France. Nor did Germany emulate Japan in developing a strong program of protection and government leadership for its electronics industries.

Although postwar Germany adopted many aspects of the American philosophy regarding the value of competition and the distrust of government economic leadership, the old German craft tradition plus a belief in cooperation with industry led the Germans to develop a variety of publicly supported institutions doing research and training for particular industries. These institutions appear to be particularly important to industries such as machine tools, where the firms are fairly small.

Summary

The industrial structures depicted in the preceding sections are far more complex than those described in any textbook on "industrial organization." These structures consist of a diverse array of public policies and programs whose instruments and objectives vary from industry to industry and from country to country. All the countries with a strong pharmaceuticals or fine chemical products industry also have a strong university research system supported by the government, but there is little direct government involvement in the development of new pharmaceuticals or direct subsidization of firms. On the other hand, in virtually all countries that have tried to support the development of electronic industries or aircraft industries, government funds flow directly to the companies, and some form of protection or preferred procurement is also provided.

The countries under discussion certainly differ in their views on the appropriate role of government in the economy. France and Japan have traditionally permitted the government to play a major entrepreneurial role, whereas the United States and Great Britain have for the most part opposed the idea of such a role for government. However, it is not ideology but rather a commitment to a strong military establishment that led governments to provide support for industrial R&D, where they did. Thus the governments of the United States and Great Britain support a far larger share of industrial R&D than does the government of Japan, and large-scale funding of industrial R&D by the French government has less to do with French notions of the appropriate entrepreneurial role of government than with the French commitment to an indigenous defense production capability.

None of the countries has put a central government office in charge of planning and coordinating industrial or technology policies across the board. Rather, each country has a diverse collection of government agencies pursuing policies that support their general mandate—

whether it be ensuring an adequate defense capability; building a nuclear electric power system or a telecommunications or health care system; or supporting agriculture. Put another way, although many governments put forth considerable rhetoric about offering policy support for high-technology industries, in fact operative policy is decentralized to a considerable extent and tied up with larger goals of the particular government where agencies concerned.

The simple stories told by economic theory about government policies needed to deal with "market failures" or to gain strategic trade advantage capture a part of the picture laid out here, but only a part. In the past decade there has been a significant increase in rhetoric that sounds like strategic trade theory and a surge in new government policies in support of high-technology industries that are expressly designed to gain international competitive advantage. These new nationalistic policies have arrived just as business is becoming increasingly transnational. The end result has been a frustration of national policies, on one hand, and a further move toward the multi-nationalization of business, on the other.

National Policies during the 1980s: Bucking the Tide of Internationalism

At the beginning of the 1980s, Japan, Europe, and the United States all faced different challenges regarding their high-tech industries. For Japan, the challenge was to devise a new set of policies now that it no longer lagged behind the United States economically and technologically. In automobiles, and memory chips, Japanese firms were producing with higher productivity and at higher levels of quality than their competitors in the United States and the rest of the world. The basic goal of Japanese technology and industrial policies since the 1960s had been to enable Japanese firms to catch up with the Americans. But the many Japanese successes had made its policies obsolete.

The major European nations—Great Britain, France, and Germany—faced a different problem. Forty years of policies that had been designed to enable European companies to catch up with the Americans had for the most part been dismal failures. With the exception of aircraft (where Airbus had succeeded on some counts), some areas of telecommunications, and sophisticated chemical products, European firms not only had not gained much ground on the Americans, but had been overtaken by the Japanese. It became clear in the late 1970s that national policies had failed, and the major European nations began to turn to the idea of intra-European cooperation.

In the 1980s the United States saw its technological and economic power rapidly eroding, and it even had lost its lead in a wide range of industries. The decline of the American textile industry, which had begun in the late 1950s, could be chalked up to the natural gravitation of low-skill, low-technology industries to developing industries. The competitive problems of the American steel industry and the automobile industry during the late 1970s were somewhat harder to take. Nevertheless, the economic future of the United States could be argued to lie in the high-tech field. But when Japanese semiconductors began pouring into the United States and several major American companies foundered, that was cause for alarm. The great challenge for the United States was to find the appropriate policies to save its high-tech future.

Japan

Japan's rise to world-class standing—first in steel, then consumer electronics, automobiles, and in the late 1970s semiconductors—and the associated surge in Japanese exports to the United States, and to a lesser degree to Europe, generated at least as much hostility abroad as respect. In fact, Japan did not run a significant current account surplus until the 1980s. Even before the 1980s, however, it was widely believed, in the United States at least, that Japan was pushing its exports and was closed to imports.

As mentioned earlier, Japanese policies of the 1960s emphasized protectionism, both in regard to its imports and its direct foreign investment. But these policies were eroded during the period of Japan's remarkable economic growth in the late 1960s and 1970s. In 1980, however, perhaps largely as a legacy of these earlier policies, Japanese imports of manufactured products were very low, as a fraction of internal consumption of manufactured products, for a country of Japan's size and income level. And, unlike Europe, and the United States after 1975, Japan had few foreign-owned manufacturing plants.

Because Japanese exports to the United States and Europe had increased, the fact that the economy still remained closed angered many other countries, particularly the United States.

Americans were also upset by (although they later came to admire) various research and development support and coordination programs organized by organs of the Japanese government, particularly MITI. The VLSI project of the late 1970s, for example, was watched very closely by the Americans and Europeans, and when the Japanese semiconductor industry became a formidable world competitor in the early 1980s, foreigners gave the project much of the credit for this success.

All the same, the Japanese argued that public funding counted for only a small fraction of total industrial R&D spending. The fraction of total industrial R&D in semiconductors and computers funded by the Japanese government was far smaller than in the United States or in the major European countries. Japanese observers acknowledged that VLSI had helped Japanese firms catch up with the Americans but stressed that most of the effort and the funding had come from the firms themselves.

According to several observers, the Japanese firms that considered themselves closest to the cutting edge of technology were somewhat aloof from the VLSI project. There was some doubt as to whether projects like VLSI would be useful or would gain the support of Japanese companies when the industry as a whole had caught up. The fifth-generation project started during the 1980s lends support to these doubts. Japanese companies have been reluctant to sink their own funds into the project. The results are often politely labeled as "disappointing."[15]

As the Japanese began catching up with the Americans, many in Japan as well as in the United States felt that the Japanese now needed to contribute to the basic knowledge and techniques that would pave the way for the next generation of products. The fifth-generation project was intended to do just that, although it was not considered successful. More attention was then given to basic research in general. Various proposals were put forth suggesting that the government step up its support for basic research at universities. Japanese companies

15. For an interesting discussion of the fifth-generation project, see Grindley, Mowery, and Silverman (1994, pp. 723–58).

themselves began to mount various efforts that they called "basic research."

In the past three or four years Japanese growth has come to a virtual standstill, and there is now little talk of companies increasing their basic research spending. In fact, the Japanese are expressing grave concern about the policies and economic structures that served them so well during the era of Japanese catch-up. Now that they have caught up, these policies no longer work.

Another important development of the 1980s was Japan's decision to respond to American and European hostility toward Japanese exports by using its huge trade surpluses to buy or build consumer electronics plants in the United States and Europe. Japanese "transplants" soon took a significant share of the U.S. automobile market, and by the late 1980s production by the transplants exceeded Japanese exports to the United States. Japanese investment in semiconductor plants in the United States and Europe, also surged.

Thus by the early 1990s Japanese-owned companies in high-tech industries were well on the road to becoming multinationals, like their counterparts in the United States and Europe.

Europe

In contrast, as the 1980s dawned in Europe, people were still trying to figure out how to catch up. Increasingly aware that national policies were not working, and that they would not be able to work without larger markets and higher levels of support, Europeans began thinking that an integrated European economy would be the only way to achieve world-class levels in high-tech industry. The Airbus experience was held up as an example of what Europeans could accomplish if they pooled and coordinated their efforts.

Under programs like ESPRIT, which focuses on "precompetitive" research, projects must have partners from two or more European countries. Similarly, Eureka requires Pan-European partnerships among firms, but it is more concerned with commercial products. In any case, these have been Europe's flagship programs in support of electronics industries during the 1980s and early 1990s.[16] The European Commission's mandate in technology policy was sharpened and

16. For a discussion of ESPRIT and Eureka, see Grindley and others (1994, pp. 723–58).

legitimated by the Single European Act of 1985. This act established the concept of the European Technology Community (ETC), which clearly is emblematic of the new faith and strategy. At the same time, the individual nations of Europe continue to have policies and objectives of their own. Thus Britain's Alvey program and the French Filiere Electronique have proceeded in parallel with ESPRIT and involved greater resources.

In an integrated economy, there is also the question of what one means by a British or a European firm. The problem can be illustrated by considering two Pan-European programs: JESSI and HDTV.

The JESSI program was designed to support European companies producing semiconductors. Partly because the American Sematech program was officially closed to all foreign subsidiaries in the United States, JESSI was originally closed to foreign-owned companies working in Europe. By forming an alliance with Siemens, however, IBM was indirectly admitted to JESSI. Siemens thereby obtained unofficial access to Sematech. The problem of foreign access to JESSI rose again in 1990 when Fujitsu bought 80 percent of ICL, the British computer firm. Although ICL was initially excluded from the governing body of JESSI, it later was readmitted on a "limited" basis. In any case, Fujitsu had been establishing a number of joint ventures with American firms, which themselves have alliances with key European firms in the computer and semiconductor industries, and which are associated with JESSI (See table 2-1).

The HDTV project was organized through Eureka to establish a new European standard for greatly enhanced transmission of audio and video information. The big European electronics firms, especially Philips, Siemens, and Thomson, clearly were interested in servicing the new equipment market themselves if at all possible and in keeping the Japanese out. This objective was explicit ETC policy. As noted above, however, the major European firms already had a number of alliances with American and Japanese firms. And in the early 1990s these connections were broadened and strengthened, notably in areas directly related to HDTV. It is now apparent that the equipment that will service HDTV in Europe, whatever the new standards turn out to be, will be provided by firms that have a home base in Europe but that are part of an international technology network (see table 2-2).

Table 2-1. *Major Semiconductor Alliances*

Alliance	Year	Agreement
IBM–Thomson–CSF	1992	Thomson–CSF will market IBM power PC microprocessor chips.
IBM–Hyundai	1991	IBM to sell some advanced memory chips to Hyundai.
IBM–Toshiba	1992	Cooperative development of SRAM.
IBM–Siemens–Toshiba	1992	Joint development, not manufacturing, 256-megabyte chip in IBM labs in United States.
IBM–Siemens	1990	Advanced DRAM cooperation; joint $700 million plant in France; cancel pact for 64-megabyte plant in 1992.
AT&T–NEC	1992	Joint venture 51 percent owned by AT&T will sell AT&T chips to Japanese companies and some systems that use chips from both firms.
	1992	Cooperate on 64-megabyte DRAM development.
	1990	AT&T CAD technology for NEC advanced logic technology.
AT&T–Mitsubishi	1990	256-K SRAM production capacity of AT&T for new SRAM technology of Mitsubishi; AT&T capacity in gallium arsenide foundry and silicon packaging for Mitsubishi. Expanded in 1992 to include microcontrollers.
Intel–Sharp	1992	Joint design, manufacturing, and development of process technology of flash memory (.6 micron); includes Sharp factory in Japan to produce Intel chips.
Intel–NMBS	1990	NMBS sources DRAMs and flash memory to Intel.
TI–Hitachi	1991	Joint development of 64-megabyte DRAM.
TI–Hyundai	1991	Hyundai manufactures 1-megabyte DRAM for TI.
TI–Kobe Steel	1990	Kobe to build TI ASIC chips.
Hitachi–Gold Star	1991	Gold Star manufactures 1-megabyte DRAM for Hitachi.
ADM–Fujitsu	1992	5 percent cross-equity swap and joint development and manufacturing of flash memory chips in joint Japanese plant.
Advanced Micro Devices (AMD)–Sony	1990	Sony buys AMD factory in United States and provides technology to AMD.
Sematech–JESSI	1991	U.S. and European research consortia agree in principle to develop memory chips jointly; implementation pending.

Table 2-1. (*continued*)

Alliance	Year	Agreement
Sematech–Ultraclean	1991	Sematech becomes member society (Japan) of Tohoku University research group, which works on semiconductor technology with 235 Japanese and 20 foreign firms.
Siemens–SGS–Thomson	1990	Cooperation to develop and sell microcontrollers.
Siemens–Toshiba	1988	Siemens licenses Toshiba 1-megabyte DRAM and CMOS technology.
Integrated Device Technology (IDT) (U.S.)–Siemens–Toshiba	1991	RISC technology; IDT RISC technology to be jointly developed and some production cooperation among the firms.[a]
Motorola–Toshiba	1986	DRAM manufacturing. Updated periodically to cover new generations.
Motorola–Philips	1990	Philips will sell Motorola's RISC's systems under an original equipment manufacturing contract.
Motorola–Philips	1992	Joint investment to build semiconductor design facility for interactive multimedia products.
NEC–MIPS	1992	To jointly develop 64-bit RISC chip.
Paradigm–NKK	1991	NKK (a steel firm) buys 10 percent of Paradigm and licenses its SRAM technology.
SGS–Thompson–Oki	1991	European DRAM manufacturing.
Sanyo–LSI–NKK	1991	LSI commits to new Japan R&D center to cooperate on HDTV chips and will manufacture with Sanyo.
Advanced Computing Environment (ACE)	1988	Firms agree to use MIPS RISC technology as base for their computer systems.[b]

Source: Cowhey and Aronson (1993, pp. 148–49). Reprinted with permission of Council on Foreign Relations Press. Copyright 1993.

a. IDT is a 1980 startup that has sales of roughly $200 million a year.

b. ACE members included MIPS, Compaq, DEC, Bull, Gold Star, and Epson.

United States

Like the Europeans, the Americans entered the 1980s fearful of the Japanese and ready to imitate them. Part of the American response, of course, has been overt protection. Automobiles and semiconductors are striking examples. In both cases, protection was justified on two counts. The Japanese market was itself preserved for Japanese firms,

Table 2-2. *Selected Alliances in High-Definition Systems and Components*

Firms	Objectives
Texas Instruments, NHK	Technology transfer, license for the design of semiconductors used in decoding for HDTV sets from NHK to TI
Texas Instruments, Sony	Use by Sony of TI's digital signal processors in new CD players
IBM, Toshiba	Joint venture to produce LCDs for next generation workstations and computers in Japan; also IBM interest in manufacturing technology from Toshiba
Xerox, Standish	Joint development agreement to explore possible manufacturing and marketing of high-resolution active-matrix displays
NBC, Philips, Thomson, David Sarnoff Research Center (DSRC)	Introduction of enhanced-resolution TV and joint development of a digital HDTV simulcast system for the United States
Zenith, AT&T	Joint development of fully digital HDTV transmission system for the United States (including HDTV receiver)
General Instrument, MIT	Joint development of fully digital HDTV transmission system

Source: Beltz (1991, p. 83). Reprinted with permission of American Enterprise Institute for Public Policy Research, Washington.

and closed to Americans, and turnabout was only fair play. Second, the Japanese industries were dumping on the American market.

The Japanese response to some of these complaints, as already mentioned, was to establish plants in the United States. The production of cars in Japanese-owned plants in the United States now significantly exceeds Japanese automobile exports to the United States, and the same holds for semiconductor products.

American attempts to develop a responsive technology policy over this period can charitably be called chaotic, even though the share of industrial R&D spending financed by the government throughout the post–World War II era has been substantially greater than that in any other country and vastly larger than that in Japan. The electronics industry has been an important recipient of these funds. Virtually all of those funds came from the Department of Defense, however, and were targeted toward military technologies. No strong case can be made that, up until the 1980s, public support was intended to help the industry do better commercially. By the early 1980s that had changed. American policy during the mid-1980s and early 1990s can best be understood as an attempt to establish support for civil technologies as a legitimate objective of government.

As in Europe, American policies have been greatly influenced by perceptions of what the Japanese were doing. In the early 1980s all eyes were on the Japanese VLSI program, and some observers complained that American semiconductor and computer companies were at a disadvantage because American antitrust laws barred such cooperative research ventures. The 1984 amendment to American antitrust law, in the form of the National Cooperative Research Act, removed from such ventures some of the threat of prosecution under antitrust. The formation of the Microelectronics and Computer Technology Corporation proceeded in parallel with the effort to reform legislation.

The new antitrust environment was the setting for the establishment of Sematech in 1987, but Sematech involved public funding as well—in this case through the Department of Defense—for a venture aimed directly at supporting the development of civilian technology. It should be noted that Sematech, like the Japanese VLSI program of a decade earlier, was expressly designed to help American firms "catch up." In this case, the technology had to do with semiconductor production processes, and the companies involved included both semiconductor production firms and equipment suppliers. Some enthusiasts saw Sematech as a new candidate for long-run precompetitive research in the field of semiconductor process technology. However, the program at Sematech has by and large focused on providing a vehicle for interaction between semiconductor producers and the producers of semiconductor production equipment, and on supporting research at that interface.[17]

The 1980s saw several other developments on the technology policy front. One was the establishment of a number of programs located at universities, which were partly funded by federal and state governments and whose express purpose was to develop technology of relevance to industry. The Engineering Research Centers, partly

17. Grindley and others (1994, pp. 723–58).

funded by the National Science Foundation, make up one set of such institutions. Structures like the North Carolina Microelectronics Center show state governments actively involved in these ventures. In general, the states became much more active in establishing programs designed to help local industry. Some of these programs were linked to universities.

The Reagan administration was basically hostile to these attempts at government involvement in the development of civilian technology. The Bush administration was somewhat more pragmatic, but hardly enthusiastic. With the end of the cold war in the late 1980s and the arrival of the Clinton administration in 1992, things changed significantly.

The Clinton administration is obviously much less skeptical than were earlier administrations about the appropriateness and potential effectiveness of government programs to help in the development of civilian technology. Furthermore, because the cold war has come to an end, the rationale for government R&D support needs to shift from military security to economic security if government support for R&D is to continue. Indeed, the new administration has committed itself, broadly, to a massive shift.

The 1994 Annual Report of the Council of Economic Advisers contains a section on "promoting technology" in which the council tries to lay out, in a coherent way, the rationale for the administration's programs in this area.[18] The economists' "market failure" language, discussed at the beginning of this chapter, is developed at some length. The report also warns against government involvement in programs that can become highly politicized or that might allow the government to make decisions for business. Despite these caveats, this administration is clearly more enthusiastic than prior ones about the idea of an active technology policy.

In fact, the policies of this administration have largely consisted of extending and augmenting the policies of earlier administrations, although there have been several new ventures. Priorities regarding government funding of basic research at universities continues the shift, begun more than a decade ago, toward trying to fund university research that is likely to feed into technical progress in industry and encouraging universities to establish closer links with industry. The

18. *Economic Report of the President* (1994, pp. 189–204).

administration has been active in encouraging industry to form cooperative research ventures, and new legislation has been passed that will allow industries to cooperate in the development and production of products that have been created through cooperative research.

The advanced technology program, administered through the National Institute of Standards and Technology, has been significantly expanded. Under this program proposals are solicited from industry in areas mapped out broadly by the institute. Proposals are then screened by an expert panel. Although public funding of industry research under this program has not as yet reached $100 million a year, the administration plans to increase its funding significantly.

Under legislation passed in the mid-1980s, the National Laboratories are authorized to participate in cooperative research projects with industry, with the laboratories and industry sharing the costs. This administration has actively been pushing this policy, and, more generally, pushing the laboratories to allocate a significantly increased share of their efforts to research of direct relevance to industry. The partnership for the new generation of vehicles, is but the tip of this iceberg.

In addition, the administration has been trying to get more Defense Department projects to focus on "dual-use" technologies, that is, on technologies that would be relevant to civilian industry as well as to the military. And a significant portion of the funds under the department's technology reinvestment project, which is aimed to help defense contractors learn to meet civilian markets, is spent in industry.

The set of programs that has been put forth thus far under the new administration seems more like a grab bag than any well thought out plan. In view of the division of R&D spending and authority across a wide range of government agencies, and other turf dividers built into the U.S. political system as it operates in this field, it seems unlikely that the United States will develop a coherent policy in support of its high-tech industries. There is every reason to believe, however, that the rhetoric will continue to promote such industries and that there will be a continuing flow of proposals for government programs to support them, a number of which will be accepted and financed.

One important indicator of how far the United States has moved down this road is the change in the U.S. position on the "fairness" of governmental subsidies for industrial research and development. Initially, the U.S. position was that any government support of R&D

designed to help civilian industry was unfair. When Europeans pointed out that the American aircraft industry had been helped enormously by military research and development and procurement contracts, the U.S. position was that that was not the principal intent of such programs. Long-standing programs of support of R&D for agriculture were argued to be, somehow, something different. Although the United States made no direct concerted attacks on European programs such as ESPRIT and Eureka, it clearly considered these to be pressing on the limits of acceptability. Over the past year, however, the United States has taken the position that support of at least precompetitive research and development is justified on "market failure" grounds. The subsidy of "commercial development and production" continues to be beyond the pale, in the U.S. view. But these lines, although easy to draw sharply on paper, are extremely blurry in practice.

High-Technology Fetishism and Technonationalism

Several observations are now in order. First, Europe and now the United States may have bought into a myth about the economic importance of having their "own" high-tech industries. The attention they have given to such industries clearly has been prompted by the slow economic growth and rising level of unemployment that these regions have experienced over the past quarter century. However, it is doubtful that the real economic problems these regions are experiencing have much to do with what is going on in high-tech, or that doing something to help high-tech will have much impact on slow growth and unemployment. Similarly, whatever is now ailing the Japanese economy probably has very little to do with whether its semiconductor industry or its computer industry have stopped catching up with, or pulling away from, the Americans. In short, their behavior may be symptomatic of what can be called high-tech fetishism.

Second, much of the current debate about technology policies is in any case naive. On one side, particularly in the United States, many influential people continue to argue that government should not be supporting the development of technology, but that this matter should be left to business alone. However, as the discussion in this chapter indicates, high-technology industries have, from their beginning, been complex structures in which public institutions such as universities and private for-profit ones such as business firms have interacted, and public support traditionally has gone to these industries in a variety of ways. The new strategic trade theorists have suggested that industries marked by large up-front R&D costs and steep learning curves are very different from the standard industries of the price theory textbooks, and they are. However, the features stressed by the strategic trade theorists are only the tip of the iceberg.

On the other side of the argument, there are those who see a need for a broad, well-coordinated, national technology policy. No country ever seems to have had one. And, in the light of the enormous differences across the various high-technology industries and the differences in the nature of the public interest in them, it is highly unlikely that any centralized policy could possibly work.

Government action "in support of" high-technology industries is nonetheless stepping up. Japan, Europe, and now the United States all seem committed to the notion that it is vital for nations to preserve and enhance their national high-technology firms. Yet, it has become less and less clear what it means to be a "Japanese" or an "American" or a "European" firm, particularly in these high-technology industries. The major companies themselves now tend to have plants, and often laboratories, located in a number of different countries, not just the home one. More and more companies themselves are linked by dense and overlapping networks of technological agreements and cooperative arrangements.

For the reasons spelled out in chapter 1, high-tech industry is in any case rapidly becoming transnational. Paradoxically, however, the new national policies have spurred this development. By closing their markets to imports, nations have encouraged foreign firms to establish branches inside their borders. Through policies of "buying national" or supporting only national firms, governments have induced firms, by location or alliance, to take on the colors of whatever nation is offering them something.

Much of what is going on appears to be foolishness, but it is not benign foolishness. The problem is that a dramatic and misconceived belief about the importance of "national" high-tech industry is now giving rise to a fractious and possibly dangerous set of disputes among the major industrial powers. This issue is the subject of chapter 3.

Chapter 3

High-Tech Conflict in the 1980s

A NUMBER of contradictions and perverse results have emerged in the trade policies of the major players striving to achieve technonationalism. During the 1980s there was a significant increase in international conflict centered on high-tech or technology-intensive products (for example, aircraft, supercomputers, telecommunications products, automobiles) and key components in systems-products sectors (for example, semiconductors). Only one of these—the dispute between the United States and the European Union over Airbus—involved subsidies, perhaps because up to then, outside of defense the amount of government funding directed to commercial design and development had been fairly small. But, as this chapter explains, the Airbus conflict may be a harbinger of the future in this area.

In addition to the Airbus dispute over subsidies, other high-tech conflicts emerged in the 1980s that may also have a long-lasting effect on trade relations and trade policy. Thus the U.S.-EU negotiations on government procurement and the market-oriented sector-specific negotiations between the United States and Japan introduced several novel concepts into trade policy: for example, that market access (either through trade or investment, or both) may be impeded by structural phenomena such as domestic regulations, institutional practices or governance arrangements, and that comparable access (that is, specific reciprocity) should be the objective of such negotiations.[1] Trade mea-

---

sures were adopted that either intentionally or inadvertently influenced investment. Thus it was that the new term *IRTMs*—investment-related trade measures—entered the lexicon of policy discourse.[2] IRTMs accelerated technoglobalism, among other things, by hastening the diffusion of enterprise innovation.

Tacit knowledge, which includes knowledge about the organization of the enterprise or the process of production, is not easily diffused across borders. It is best diffused through continuous observation or actual participation in the process, and thus the best diffusion channel is foreign direct investment. The export of "Fordism" from the United States to Europe was, as noted by Servan-Schreiber, the export of the management techniques of mass production. But *IRTMs* was not the only term to be added to the trade policy vocabulary. The U.S.-Japanese dispute over semiconductors had to do with the management of results in the form of voluntary import expansion, or *VIEs*. A direct descendant of VIEs is the focus on quantitative indicators in the U.S.-Japanese Framework negotiations launched by the Clinton administration in 1993. Finally, the dispute in the late 1980s that led to the U.S.-Japanese initiative pertaining to structural impediments expanded the idea of structural barriers to include a wide range of domestic (macro and micro) policies, regulations, institutions, and practices. The U.S.-Japanese Framework negotiations have carried forward this all-embracing approach. Although a full account of these numerous and complex trade disputes are beyond the scope of this discussion, a selective presentation is useful in order to highlight the interrelationship between the issues raised at the outset of this book (the erosion of U.S. dominance, the rise of Japan, technoglobalism and technonationalism) and the policy discussion in chapter 4.[3]

---

establish that domestic policy measures affect international trade. This idea was further extended in the Uruguay Round, which includes trade-related intellectual property measures, trade-related investment measures, and trade in services. In the case of services, it is entirely domestic regulation that affects both trade and investment.

2. See United Nations (1992, pp. 267–72). IRTMs were not confined to high-tech sectors. Rules of origin, which in some respects are disguised investment measures in regional trade agreements, for example, have an across-the-board effect.

3. For a detailed presentation of many of the specific disputes, see Tyson (1992); and Bergsten and Noland (1993).

The Subsidies Dispute: Airbus

In one sense, the American attack on Airbus reflects the commercial spillover of postwar American subsidization and procurement in the defense industry and the European response to that phenomenon. But, as suggested in chapter 4, conflict over high-tech subsidies may escalate in the future now that the U.S. policy stance in multilateral negotiations has shifted from seeking to eliminate R&D subsidies in other countries to promoting support for commercial research and development.

American preeminence in commercial aircraft after World War II was, as described earlier, at least partly the result of spillover from vast expenditures on military research and development and government procurement contracts. The European Airbus project, by contrast, although it had some security rationale in its early days, was a purely commercial endeavor by the time it finally took off in the early 1980s.[4] Between 1980 and 1985 the A300 captured 50 percent of all orders for wide-bodied jets. At this time, U.S. exports were still suffering from the serious blow dealt by the OPEC oil shocks, the slowdown in economic growth, and the overvalued dollar. Friction mounted when Airbus launched the more advanced A320 and secured orders from major Boeing customers. (Today Airbus has a market share of about one-third of large aircraft, which is about half that of the dominant producer, Boeing.) From 1986 to 1992, amid heated charges and countercharges, the United States and the European Union sought to renegotiate the 1979 GATT on trade in civil aircraft. The major sticking point concerned subsidies.

A plausible rationale for the European support of Airbus is that because of economies of scale and scope, as well as dynamic learning economies, Boeing was well on the road toward a global monopoly on large commercial aircraft. Without government support, the barriers to entry were such that the market was not contestable. So the government subsidies were, in effect, an antimonopoly policy designed to increase consumer welfare. In addition, it can be argued that this is a "strategic" industry, in both the military sense and in the sense that it provides good jobs (rent shifting), favorable effects on the

4. For the history of Airbus, see Scherer (1992, pp. 67–73); and Nelson (1984, pp. 52–56).

terms of trade and technological spillover. A number of studies of Airbus, however, have failed to resolve the debate about either consumer welfare or rent shifting.[5]

However, the Airbus conflict was not over whether subsidies to the aircraft industry are good or bad economics—both sides subsidized, even though the United States would not admit this—but how to constrain their use without creating an "unfair" advantage to one side or the other. The original American policy goal in the mid-1960s—to eliminate all trade-distorting subsidies (which implied a denial of American indirect industrial policy stemming from defense expenditure and procurement)—gave way to technical haggling over definitions and measurement issues. The April 1992 agreement established limits on both direct and indirect (military) subsidies for the *development* of a new aircraft, while banning all *production* support and limiting other forms of government support such as interest charges on loans for Airbus.[6]

The 1992 bilateral agreement had taken six years of negotiation, which indicated just how difficult it was to grapple with the question of whether the government should support research and development. Granted there were unique circumstances in the aircraft sector, the jewel in the crown of America's technological prowess, not least of which was the discrepancy between indirect and direct industrial policy. But it is not just the aircraft industry that has problems reaching an effective international agreement on R&D subsidies, as can be seen from the discussion of the Uruguay Round subsidies code in chapter 4.

Indeed, the Airbus conflict was by no means settled by the 1992 agreement. Recent efforts to multilateralize and extend the bilateral accord have reopened the U.S.-EU arguments about the measurement of subsidies, with each side charging the other of a lack of transparency. Furthermore, the European Union has expressed concern about proposals to create an aeronautic technology consortium designed to increase government support for civil aircraft research. The argument that such support will be at the precompetitive and generic level of technology development, which would distinguish it from "things like Airbus," according to the assistant to the president

5. For a review of some of these analyses, see Tyson (1992, pp. 192–95).
6. See "Special Report, U.S.-E.C. Agreement on Government Support for Civil Aircraft," *Inside U.S. Trade,* April 10, 1992.

for science and technology, may be easier said than codified.[7] But it also reflects the dramatic eleventh-hour turnaround in American policy on subsidies in the GATT negotiations. The allowable limits on both basic and applied research subsidies demanded by American negotiators and reflected in the so-called Dunkel Draft of December 1991 were significantly increased in the final stages of the negotiations in December 1993. In addition, the definition of applied research was expanded to include precompetitive activity. The European Union announced that this change satisfied its demand that "development" be included in applied research (for example, Airbus). This request was immediately denied by the U.S. commerce undersecretary. Le plus ça change. . . .

Disputes over Government Procurement and Regulation of Standards

Both the dispute with the European Union over public procurement of telecommunications equipment and the market-oriented sector-specific (MOSS) negotiations with Japan (which included a number of high-tech products) illustrate, albeit in different ways, the emergence of the concept of structural impediments. In both these negotiations, the disputes centered on the role of government and the interface between governments and private agents. Since there are significant differences between the systems of governance in the United States and Europe, on the one hand, and between the U.S. and Japanese systems, on the other, the notion of structural impediments reflected the emerging American view that these very broad and fundamental differences in systems were unfair barriers to access. This idea was further expanded in the U.S.-Japan semiconductor dispute and Structural Impediments Initiative, discussed later in the chapter.

The dispute between the United States and the European Community over government procurement practices affecting telecommunications and heavy electrical equipment goes back to the 1970s, and it led to the Tokyo Round Government Purchasing Agreement in 1979. The code was limited in that its definitions were too general and

7. "Senior EC Officials Raise Specter of U.S. Violations of Bilateral Aircraft Deal," *Inside U.S. Trade,* March 19, 1993, p. 5.

it covered only central government purchases. Utilities, and thus telecommunications, were excluded. During the 1980s, the deregulation of the U.S. telecommunications industry opened up the American market in terminal equipment, and foreign imports increased. This evoked complaints of a lack of reciprocity and demands by Congress for retaliatory action against European firms such as Siemens. Finally, the administration included in the 1988 Omnibus Trade Act a provision on sectoral reciprocity in telecommunications that required reports to Congress on market access. In its 1989 report, the European Union was identified as a "priority country" and negotiations were launched. The parties failed to reach a satisfactory agreement, with the result that the United States imposed sanctions in mid-1993, which were quickly followed by European sanctions.[8]

The dispute over telecommunications illustrates that fundamental differences in the role, behavior, and even the structure of government can have a significant impact on market access in the procurement area. In contrast with most public utilities in the European countries, those in the United States are either state-owned or private and regulated. In the negotiations the United States sought to exclude state purchases and private regulated utilities. The European Utilities Directive, enacted in January 1993, opened up bids for equipment in all member countries but with local content and price preference provisions (which, since the GATT codes do not cover utilities, was not in violation of international rules). The United States argued that the directive was discriminatory, that the U.S. market was "the most open in the world," and that U.S. firms "do not have comparable shares of the EC market."[9] The Europeans argued that Buy America provisions at the state level were barriers to access, as was the American refusal to include private, regulated firms. EU telecommunications firms, by contrast, are still largely government owned and come under the Utilities Directive. Both sides were arguing for reciprocity. But the systemic differences made it extremely difficult to achieve that objective.

One of the provisions under Europe 1992 (the completion of the internal market) was that the Europeans would attempt to reduce the

8. For a detailed account of the long-running dispute over public procurement, see Woolcock (1992, pp. 85–91).

9. See *International Trade Reporter* (1993, p. 527).

impact of differing regulatory policies as barriers to trade and investment. The "new approach," codified in the Single European Act, sought to achieve minimal harmonization of regulatory practices and standards and required member states to mutually recognize each other's practices. Mutual recognition implies a degree of regulatory divergence, not full harmonization, and the principle of mutual recognition required "home state" control of regulatory practices. This major breakthrough in market opening in Europe was the driving force behind the EU shift to the concept of reciprocity. Although the United States reacted angrily to the first public pronouncement of the idea of reciprocity (in banking), because many American financial service companies took it as the first signal of the "fortress Europe" philosophy, which would feed similar protectionist pressures in the U.S. Congress, the objective of reciprocity in access for telecommunications was written into the 1988 Trade Act.[10] However, the principle of mutual recognition and its corollary, regulation by the country of incorporation or "home-state rule," in EU parlance, were anathema to the United States. Although the U.S. Constitution probably would permit the federal government to exercise authority over Buy America legislation at the state level, American negotiators have consistently refused to include state laws in discussions of government procurement. (Thus, for example, the principle of national treatment and *host* government control is fundamental to the provisions on technical barriers to trade and regulation in the North American Free Trade Agreement to preserve national sovereignty.) Overcoming other systemic differences, such as the role of private sector utilities versus government purchasing, is probably easier than tackling the fundamental issues in federalism and the concept of national sovereignty. If mutual recognition and home-state rule are unacceptable, as the U.S. position implies, the logical options that remain are full regulatory harmonization or quantitative market share targets. There is some element of both these alternatives in the American policy posture toward Japan. As Yogi Berra said: "When you come to a crossroad, take it."

10. The idea of reciprocity in banking was included in a speech by former Commissioner de Clerq in July 1988. Reaction was so strong that the European Community issued a "clarification" to the Draft Second Banking Directive in October. See Croham (1989). The phrase "comparable, effective and lasting access" is used in the European Community Utilities Directive.

In the mid-1980s the United States launched the market-oriented sector-specific negotiations with Japan. These included a number of technology-intensive products such as medical equipment, pharmaceuticals, supercomputers, and telecommunication equipment. As was illustrated by the conflict with the European over government procurement of telecommunications, the importance of the MOSS talks was that they were to add to the evolving U.S. trade agenda government regulatory practices as structural impediments to effective access, either by trade or investment, for such products. In addition, access to technology through participation in publicly funded Japanese R&D consortia was raised for the first time on a trade agenda.

The barriers identified in the negotiations included the Japanese approach to standard setting and product testing (it focused on design more than on performance and was less transparent); the relations between Japanese producers and government departments in regulatory procedures and in standards and certification; and the weakness of antitrust regulations in public procurement or their nonenforcement.

The American goal in these negotiations was to ensure that regulatory practices were in harmony with the American viewpoint, which tends to favor more performance orientation and an explicit statutory approach, which is legalistic and transparent. Thus transparency is a basic characteristic of the American system, which is more legalistic than that of either Japan or the EU, and thus requires regulatory barriers to be precisely defined by statute. This legalism also emphasizes due process and the private rights of enforcement, another distinctive feature of the American system. Design orientation is often more intrusive and calls for closer collaboration between government bodies and the private sector. Along the same lines, another objective of the Americans was to establish independent agencies for standards, testing, and certification and to include American representation on these agencies and boards to reduce the possibility of collusion between government agencies and domestic firms, which might try to use technical barriers to impede market access. Finally, the issue of antitrust enforcement brought to light another structural impediment, involving not what government *does* but what it *does not do*.

Although these disputes illustrate that system differences do exist between the United States and the European Union, as well as the

United States and Japan, the *transatlantic* conflict over high-technology during the 1980s was limited to specific sectors and was more or less contained. The same was not true of the U.S.-Japanese relationship, probably for a variety of reasons, including a more striking asymmetry of access, especially in investment, which, as emphasized in the discussion of globalization in the 1980s, also affects trade.[11] The twinning of trade and investment was, indeed, hastened by the use of IRTMs, in both the European Community and the United States during the 1980s.

Investment-Related Trade Measures

The impact of IRTMs (that is, the use of trade measures to induce investment) can be illustrated by the EU experience with antidumping action and managed trade in the electronics sector. Whereas the investment consequences of trade policy are often unintended by the policymakers (the U.S. voluntary export restraint agreements (VERs) concerning automobiles is an example discussed below), this seems not to be the case in Europe. Even though trade action is hardly an ideal instrument for industrial policy, there seems little doubt that the Europeans adapted their managed trade and antidumping regulations for that purpose.

As described in chapter 2, the electronics industry, long the concern of national policy in many European countries, has been at the center of European industrial policy since the early 1980s, after the disappointing results, especially in France, of fostering "national champions." In large part, the policy was propelled by the fear of Japanese competition and its possible global dominance in consumer electronics and critical components. The rationale for preserving a European industry included the arguments of externalities, good jobs, and Japanese "industrial targeting." Although Community programs were developed to foster the European electronics industries, in some sectors the Japanese had moved too far and too fast for the Europeans to find any plausible means of catching up. The only realistic way to

---

11. The effects of twinning investment and trade are not only economic. Woolcock (1992, p. 25) makes this point very strongly. The presence of European companies in the United States and American companies in Europe also constrains political rhetoric and action in trade disputes.

secure a European presence in such sectors was to replace Japanese exports with Japanese production.

The first example of this approach has to do with videocassette recorders (VCRs) and the famous Poitiers episode of 1982.[12] By forcing all imports through a small, remote, and understaffed customs post (Poitiers) and using the threat of antidumping action, the Europeans finally triggered negotiations with the Japanese. These negotiations established the first European VERs in 1982. By including in the VERs limited quotas on components (to limit the number of plants that simply assembled imported kits of components or "screwdriver" plants) and by engaging in a good deal of backroom negotiation, Europeans pressed for local content. As a result, exports from Japan declined, Japanese VCR production in Europe expanded rapidly, and Japanese market share increased dramatically. At the same time, all European VCR producers licensed Japanese technology and formed joint ventures with Japanese companies. The VCRs manufactured by European firms use Japanese or Asian parts and quite possibly have less local content than the Japanese firms in Europe, so it would be difficult to answer the question "Who's us?" for a firm and "Who made this?" for a product. Near the end of the decade, as Korean VCR exports into Europe expanded, antidumping threats and VERs encouraged the larger Korean producers to follow the Japanese lead.

One of the arguments used to promote protection of the consumer electronics industry was that this was necessary to preserve a market for semiconductors, a key component in a range of products. Here again, the Europeans feared Japanese dominance stemming from industrial targeting.

The structure of the Japanese industry, which is made up of large, vertically integrated electronics firms, not only provided an internal market and an incentive to increase production in order to capture dynamic learning efficiencies but also the opportunity to cross-subsidize the production of components. Moreover, because of vertical integration, Japanese dominance in semiconductors also threatened the main European user industries, especially computers.

In the course of the VCR negotiations, European backroom policy to limit screwdriver plants was made explicit by a change in anti-dumping regulations in 1987, designed, in effect, to increase local

---

12. See Tyson (1992, pp. 219–37).

content by redefining the rules of origin.[13] (The negotiations on local content in the automobile sectors that sought to preclude Japanese suppliers did not involve formal changes in rules of origin.) The next year dumping investigations against Japanese semiconductor producers were initiated, and they were settled in 1989 by an agreement to set floor prices. This elicited vociferous complaints from users: to no avail. Predictably, however, the dumping action triggered a marked increase in both Japanese and American semiconductor investment, creating spillover friction with the United States as American plants moved into Europe to protect the erosion of their market share by the Japanese.[14]

Trade policy can be used as investment policy in the European Union because the policymaking process in the area of trade is less transparent and less legalistic there than in the United States. This opacity and bureaucratic power provide considerable leeway for administrative discretion by the Commission and for behind-the-scenes lobbying both by companies and member countries.[15] In one sense, the policy was successful: Japanese investment in the European Union, mainly autos and electronics, increased from $564 million in 1980 to $14.7 billion in 1990.[16] But this very lack of transparency, as well as the manipulation of one policy instrument to achieve the implicit objectives of another, makes it impossible to evaluate the outcome *in national terms*. In *international* terms, IRTMs are clearly undesirable, since they distort investment decisions and create negative spillovers for other countries. (Among the more serious consequences of distortion is the creation of global overcapacity, already apparent in the automobile industry.) Yet in the competition for "good" investment in a globalizing world, more and more countries are likely to employ IRTMs.

The case of the American VERs on Japanese autos, first established in the early 1980s, yields other lessons about the use of IRTMs.

13. Ostry (1990, p. 48). Subsequently, a number of other changes in the definition of rules of origin were designed to induce investment in the electronics sector (Ostry 1990, pp. 49–50).

14. Tyson (1992, p. 150); and Ostry (1990, p. 49).

15. For a more detailed comparison of the process of trade policymaking in the United States and the European Community, see Ostry (1990, chap. 2). Recent changes in European Community antidumping procedures will make the process more transparent and more speedily administered.

16. OECD (1990, p. 52, table 14).

Initially intended to provide short-term relief that would allow the domestic industry to improve competitiveness, numerous studies have suggested a consistently negative evaluation in terms of costs to consumers and third-country effects on trade, and so on. The VERs were *not* disguised investment policy: indeed, a proposal to attract Japanese investment and impose domestic content provisions was put forward by the United Auto Workers but "strenuously opposed" by the administration.[17]

An unintended consequence of the VERs was that they attracted Japanese investment. Japanese plants were set up almost immediately following the first VER, initially as assembly operations but with increasing local content over time. Some Japanese parts suppliers also moved into the United States and the Japanese keiretsu became part of the transplant. Between 1985 and 1992 Japanese transplants increased production from just under 400,000 to over 2,000,000 units, and Japanese market share increased significantly. Current estimates of excess capacity in the North American auto market in the 1990s run at 2 to 3 million vehicles; these figures are more than matched in Europe.[18] Of course, global glut is a spawning ground for protectionist pressure.

Despite increasing local content, the bilateral deficit in automobile parts continued to grow and it, in turn, fueled the U.S.-Japanese trade conflict, as evidenced by President George Bush's January 1992 visit to Japan, where a numerical target for Japan's purchase of automobile parts was negotiated, and it became clear that automobiles and automobile parts would be an important topic in the U.S.-Japanese Framework discussions launched by the Clinton administration in the summer of 1993. In this case, instead of defining local content in terms of *territory*, as in Europe, there is growing pressure to define it in terms of *ownership*, partly in response to the transplanted keiretsu.

17. See Low (1993, p. 116). For a review of the evaluation of auto VERs, see OECD (1993d, pp. 59–69).

18. For North American estimates, see OECD (1992a, p. 59). See also Done (1993, p. 11) for an estimate of 10 million vehicles at a world level, with Europe facing "particularly severe" problems. The estimates of European overcapacity range from 2 million to 3.5 million cars a year during the 1990s. Japanese production in Britain is expected to reach 1 million cars a year by the end of the 1990s when the VERs are supposed to be dropped. See the *Economist* (1994, pp. 19–20).

Autos and the Keiretsu

Thus the U.S.-Japanese conflict over auto parts concerned not only the trade deficit but also the role of the Japanese vertical keiretsu, both in Japan and in its transplanted form in the Unites States. Governed by long-term, reciprocal, contractual relations, the vertical keiretsu and the Japanese method of "lean production" are highly efficient, but the keiretsu has exclusionary consequences. This issue is discussed at greater length in chapter 4, since it has moved to the center of the U.S.-Japanese debate. But staying with the auto sector at present, the Japanese model of production proved to be not only highly efficient, but also exportable. A case study of Japanese transplants in the United States undertaken by the McKinsey Global Institute is worth quoting:

> *Why is Japan so productive?* Two factors appear to be fundamental. First, the way companies organize their processes, labor, and communication within their plants and with their suppliers is important. Organizational principles such as integration, continuous improvement and supplier management are methods by which higher labor productivity is achieved. Second, the way products are designed for ease of manufacturability and assembly affects productivity. All of these traits are epitomized in Toyota. . . .
>
> *Why has the U.S. drawn close?* First, the U.S. benefits from substantial Japanese transplant production.[19]

Foreign direct investment is the best means of acquiring the "tacit knowledge" involved in the production process and the principles of enterprise organization. This transfer of knowledge can occur in many areas of industry, not only automobile assembly. Similar organizational principles are transferred to the parts suppliers who are continuously involved in the design of a vehicle and thus are encouraged to invest in training and specialized machinery. The improved productivity of the American Big Three producers, in comparison with the lagging performance in the German automobile industry, has been shown to be related to the presence of direct competition from Japanese transplants. Similar marked improvements in productivity

19. McKinsey Global Institute (1993).

occurred in the United Kingdom, where Japanese transplants were also welcomed.[20]

In sum, the auto VERs in the United States became—unintentionally—an investment policy that facilitated the diffusion of Toyotism, thus accelerating technoglobalism. This benefited the American-owned companies. But the U.S.-Japanese conflict over automobiles was not ameliorated: it simply changed focus. This continuing friction revealed the increasingly close relationship between the American automobile companies and the American government in forming trade policy. In the semiconductor dispute with Japan, discussed next, this shift to an ownership concept of domestic content is also apparent.

Voluntary Import Expansion

The U.S.-Japanese semiconductor dispute echoes, in some respects, the European concern with a "strategic" component and with the growing Japanese dominance arising from industrial targeting and a protected home market. But it also represents a new, particularly American thrust, that is, *results-oriented* negotiations designed to ensure a specified market share in Japan, or voluntary import expansion (VIE). In large part this development in the mid-1980s reflected the American situation described in chapter 1, that is, the relative decline of the United States in an important high-tech sector. Unlike the Europeans, Americans had been the unchallenged leader in the semiconductor industry, which had originated in the Bell Laboratories after World War II. The growing power of the Japanese industry challenged American dominance at home and in third-country markets. In addition, because economies of scale and scope are so important in this sector and R&D costs increasingly burdensome, access to the large and growing Japanese market was considered important in maintaining competitiveness, although the size of the U.S. and global markets makes this factor difficult to assess. The vertically integrated

20. Oliver and Wilkinson (1988). Ironically, the BMW takeover in February 1994 of the Rover Group (partly owned by Honda) was prompted by the turnaround in productivity due largely to Honda's technology and manufacturing prowess. Volkswagen is now sourcing components in the United Kingdom, partly for cost (exchange rate) reasons but also because "the components industry is also thought to have benefited in quality terms from its links with Japanese factories in the U.K." Griffiths (1994).

structure of Japanese industry made it extremely difficult for American merchant firms to export to the Japanese market. Moreover, access was impeded by barriers to trade and investment.[21] Finally, it was argued that such entry, not just by trade but also by investment, was essential to prevent collusive predatory behavior among Japanese producers that would lead to a monopoly in key sectors of the market.[22]

As was the case in Europe, the U.S.-Japanese conflict in semi-conductors began with a series of antidumping actions that led to a bilateral negotiation culminating in the Semiconductor Trade Agreement (STA) in 1986. The original agreement had several novel features: it called for the monitoring of third-party markets, in recognition of the global span of the Japanese industry, and it established a numerical target for foreign market share. The effect of price and production monitoring by MITI was to create a Japanese cartel, which greatly increased the profits of the Japanese producers and harmed all non-Japanese downstream users, including the U.S. computer industry, which had strongly opposed this aspect of the original agreement.[23] Moreover, the creation of the cartel indeed opened the door to the possibility of collusive predatory behavior: another example of the "law of unintended consequences." The five-year renewal of the STA in 1991 dropped the monitoring provisions, but a market share target for 1992 (which had only been in a confidential side letter in 1986) was reaffirmed. By the fourth quarter of 1992, that target was achieved, but by 1993 the share had again dropped below target. It is important to note that the target was defined in terms of foreign (that is, not just American) share, but that the definition of "foreign" was not the *country* of origin but the nationality of the *company*. This reflected, as in the automobile parts dispute, the successful lobbying efforts of the American producers.[24]

The VIE approach has been defended on the grounds that a combination of public and private practices have seriously impeded

21. For discussion of investment access, see Encarnation (1992). See pp. 60–61 for an account of Texas Instruments' difficulties in establishing a presence in Japan.

22. See Flamm (1993, pp. 249–333).

23. Flamm (1993, pp. 279–84). Also, Flamm, "Semiconductors," in Hufbauer, ed. (1990, pp. 248–57). The Europeans filed a successful complaint in GATT on the pricing provisions of the STA and then negotiated their own price agreement with Japan.

24. Motorola, Intel, and Texas Instruments benefited most from the STA by increased sales either from East Asian or Japanese subsidiaries. See Tyson (1992, p. 130).

access to the Japanese market, either by trade or investment. It is argued that these impediments to access in a sector with significant scale and learning economies create a credible threat of global market dominance, possibly through strategic behavior with monopolizing intent. Thus, it is argued by proponents of the results-oriented approach, that opening up the Japanese market to foreign suppliers increases competition and hence global welfare.[25] The (usually) implicit argument in this rationale is that in Japan structural barriers to access are either too complex or too time-consuming to eradicate by negotiation and therefore the bilateral VIE may be the only practical and effective approach to counter market dominance. That is to say, the concept of structural impediments implies a logic of results-oriented trade policy. (Another alternative, also proposed by some proponents of the STA, is domestic high-tech policy, which refers to the subsidy of American producers to counter the threat of foreign monopoly.)

The obvious danger of the VIE is that it is likely to give rise to international cartels and international market-sharing arrangements that would seriously undermine the liberal multilateral trading system, especially if it is "captured" by powerful firms that are the most effective lobbyists, a not unlikely possibility in the United States, as noted earlier. But the precedent set by the STA was an important one, and the successful achievement of the target at the end of 1992 served to reinforce the view in some quarters of the American business community that VIEs are both effective and desirable. Thus, for example, the first report to the Clinton administration of the high-level Advisory Committee for Trade Policy and Negotiations recommended using "temporary quantitative indicators" in sectors where "invisible barriers" exist and focusing on increased market access for "strategic" sectors.[26] And, as noted, the U.S.-Japanese Framework negotiations have stressed the use of quantitative measures.

25. Bergsten and Noland (1993, p. 142). They also propose other policy alternatives to achieve this end, including domestic high-tech policy. See also Tyson (1992, pp. 133–35). Flamm also suggests that monopolistic control in this sector would better be countered by subsidizing domestic production (1993, p. 323).

26. Report of the Advisory Committee for Trade Policy and Negotiations (1993, p. 2). A similar view was put forward by the U.S. Council on Competitiveness. It proposed a new U.S. strategy toward Japan based on results-oriented pacts because "its structural barriers and discriminatory private-sector linkages are often more entrenched than in other parts of the world" (Dunne, 1993, p. 5).

Structural Impediments and System Friction

At the end of the decade, the confrontation with Japan—in part the result of increasing American frustration with the sectoral negotiations and the MOSS—led to an entirely new approach, which vastly expanded the concept of structural barriers to access to include broader, generic macro and micro policies. The context of the Structural Impediments Initiative was the bilateral trade deficit with Japan. Thus the Japanese insisted that American fiscal policy be placed on the agenda, as well as policies related to savings behavior. But micro policy was at the heart of the American agenda, which included, among other topics, regulation of the Japanese distribution system, land-use policy, competition policy with a focus on the keiretsu, investment policies, and patent law standards and enforcement. The reciprocity concept was expanded to cover trade, investment, and technology. The range of the dispute was so broad and complex that it deserved a new name—system friction. It did not end in the 1980s. Many of the same issues, both macro and micro, were raised in the Clinton administration's Framework talks with Japan, as were sectoral numerical targets.

Chapter 4

Coping with System Friction: Deeper Integration and Other Means

*T*HE PICTURE emerging from the preceding chapters is one of increasing internationalization of private technology policies, while government technology policies remain overwhelmingly national. This trend has generated new sources of international friction and new dilemmas for policymakers. Two of the questions they now face are of particular concern. First, what are the implications of increasing technoglobalism for national and international public policies? Second, where do public policies need wider and deeper integration, and what other new approaches are required to reduce system friction?

Some Implications of Technoglobalism

National borders now mean far less than they used to as barriers for containing technology for several reasons. First, the sharp increase in international trade in high-technology products has made these products available even in countries that do not have firms to produce them. Moreover, in countries with a high level of scientific and technical sophistication, access to and familiarity with the products generate a considerable amount of understanding about them and the technology they incorporate. Thus there is some security against being denied these products. Second, business itself has grown increasingly transnational, in some industries through overseas direct investments and in others through a network of intercorporate agree-

79

ments. Third, partly as a result of the above, but partly as a force in its own right, scientific and technological communities have become transnational. Scientists and engineers trained in the United States, Japan, or Europe but working largely in their own home countries now know pretty much the same things. There are few technological "secrets" that can be kept privy for very long from professionals who are knowledgeable in the field.

For U.S. companies that used to rule the roost in high-technology industries, there have been several consequences. First, competition has become wider, and stronger. In many of these industries American firms have been forced to run faster and to innovate more rapidly and effectively, in order to stay competitive. Many have been forced not only to increase their R&D spending but also to monitor a much wider range of competitors just to stay abreast of developments in their industry, much less to keep ahead. Second, these companies are finding it more and more difficult to prevent their competitors from learning about what they are doing and developing a clone or a substitute quickly. Spillovers are much greater than they used to be and occur more quickly, at least among firms that have made the major investments to keep up with the field.

As mentioned earlier, American firms have been making several responses to these developments. To begin with, they have been requesting protection and subsidies. They are also trying to enforce intellectual property rights more forcefully. Recently, however, requests for foreign market share based on reciprocal access has become a rallying cry. Indeed, the concept of reciprocity—or a reduction of the asymmetry of access—has now become an important policy objective for some countries. The alliances formed in the 1980s by multinationals from all countries with other firms are continuing to operate, and new ones are appearing everywhere. Both trade and domestic technology policies had the unintended effect of increasing such alliances. An interesting question is whether these new cooperative arrangements increase or control global competition in high-tech industries. The answer is probably that they do some of both. How policymakers might deal with these and other issues arising from the conundrums posed by increased globalization is the central concern of this chapter.

Deeper Integration: Harmonization and Other Approaches to Reduce System Friction

The pressure for governments to harmonize domestic policies and practices stems from several sources. As already noted, when the role of the multinational enterprise (MNE) expands and there is increasing integration of global production, corporations begin pressing for more uniform regulatory policies so that they can reduce transaction costs. At the same time, governments begin to fear the loss of "footloose" firms no longer tied to natural endowments or protected local markets. Another powerful push for harmonization stems from governments (often responding to business lobbies) concerned about fairness (the level playing field), and from the international spillover of domestic policies. Because both trade and investment are essential to corporate competitiveness in high-tech sectors, the theme of the level playing field has introduced the concept of reciprocity, enshrined in the General Agreement on Tariffs and Trade (GATT), to investment and technology, as well as trade.

But perhaps the strongest push for harmonization in recent years has arisen in response to the decline of American hegemony and the rise of Japan as a new and powerful actor in high-tech sectors. This push comes primarily from Americans who argue that the pervasive and complex rivalries in high-tech are, in essence, rivalries among different capitalist systems and therefore are symptomatic of system friction. One way to reduce system friction and achieve a level playing field is to harmonize in order to establish only one brand of capitalism. This suggestion has been particularly directed toward Japan, not necessarily because the Japanese system is so different from, say, the German or the French, but mainly because the question of structural asymmetry of access in trade, investment, and technology has loomed so large in U.S.-Japanese bilateral negotiations. Whereas in both the European Community and the United States, the presence of foreign firms acts to constrain the escalation of political rhetoric and action, in Japan there are far fewer foreign voices to be heard.

The United States has a vital role to play in launching and feeding the evolutionary trend to deep integration, however vague that concept remains. This is so not only because of the rivalry with Japan, which set the scene for the high-tech conflicts of the 1980s, but also for a broader set of reasons. The idea of fair competition is a much more potent political force in the United States than elsewhere. It is deeply rooted in American history and ideology, embedded in the American Constitution, and exemplified in the antitrust laws.[1] Furthermore, the view that there can be only one "legitimate" capitalist model—the American model—also stems from historical and cultural roots as well as the enormous size, power, and self-sufficiency of the United States. Whereas Europeans are well aware of the significant variations in both economic and political systems and the need, however difficult and tedious, to work out ways of adapting to divergence, most Americans focus their attention on fairness, legitimacy, and singularity, all intertwined and deeply held convictions.

Thus one important implication of an American-led push for deep integration is a propensity to unilateralism in two senses: a unilateral view of the harmonization model and a willingness, if necessary, to use unilateral tactics to achieve the "best" results. It also follows that if harmonization is not possible, or is too tiresome and frustrating to pursue, numerical targets may be the only feasible alternatives. This would be an acceptable second-best solution for both the United States and the world, although the risk of political capture by industrial interests is recognized. The pressures for unilateralism and results-oriented negotiations have been amplified by the activities of Japan, which to date has proved unwilling or unable to take a lead in tackling impediments to access, either by vigorous and sustained domestic structural reform or multilateral initiatives. Although the European Union has criticized sectoral targets, it is unlikely to stand aside if the United States persists in such an approach. Hence one not improbable and paradoxical outcome of the current drive for deep integration would be the cartelization of high-tech sectors. This would hardly produce system convergence.

More likely, however, at least over the foreseeable future, there would be continuing bilateral friction, continuing use of unilateralism (even if ruled out in a strict legal sense by the new World Trade Organization), and thus a continuing erosion of the transparent, rule-based multilateral system. Over the long run, the chief benefit of that system has been predictability and stability, which included

---

1. For a comprehensive account of the concept of fair competition, see Hudec (1990).

restraint on cross-linkage, that is, the use of trade policy to achieve political objectives. The loss of these international public goods in an increasingly interdependent world would be serious in the extreme.

Given the strong pressures for harmonization and new forms of managed trade in high-tech sectors, one objective of international policy could simply be damage control, since the likelihood of serious destabilization in the absence of multilateral policy initiatives is high. An argument is often made—and with some considerable validity—that locational competition and rules arbitrage by MNEs will, over time, result in a marketlike process of harmonization, which need not require any intergovernmental action. This natural or marketlike process of gradual convergence is also preferable, so this argument goes, because diversity among innovation systems is in itself desirable, for it stimulates innovation and growth. Thus there should be little need for damage control, except to tackle negative spillovers, promote mutual recognition where possible, and initiate a process of explicit harmonization (the most interventionist, centralized, and therefore most difficult international policy approach) only where considered essential to sustain and reinforce the transparent multilateral rule-based system. There is a clear danger that a push to harmonize "everything" could involve a wholesale rejection of the principle of comparative advantage. The damage control proposals discussed below are presented in light of both these difficulties and dangers. They focus on multilateral—or, rather, plurilateral—approaches because although similar developments are feasible at a regional level, it is essential to include at least Europe, North America, and Japan in all discussions, and no regional arrangement at present covers all three blocs.

Harmonization

Options for harmonization include: R&D subsidies, by bringing foreign-owned firms into government-funded research consortia, and intellectual property rights. One can probably be modestly hopeful about the prospects for harmonization in the first and second and optimistic in the third.

R&D SUBSIDIES AND RESEARCH CONSORTIA.   Until recently the U.S. government tended to take a relatively simple line regarding what kinds of government R&D spending or subsidy were fair and what kinds were not. Government support of "basic research" was completely fair. On the other hand government funding of industrial applied research and development, where the objective was to help firms create new commercial products and processes, most certainly was not. Of course, governments could fund industrial R&D if the objective were to create new products or technologies of use to the military. Commercial spillover from such projects was, well, just one of those things. Also, government funding of applied research and development to improve agricultural technology was, somehow, quite acceptable. So also, for a while at least, was the funding of R&D on nuclear power. But these complications tended to get pushed aside in statements of general principles. Here the position was that funding of basic research was fair, but that anything that subsidized commercial technological development was not.

A rather dramatic change in the American position occurred when the Clinton administration came to power. No longer was a sharp line drawn between basic and applied research. And support of industrial research and development was no longer a no-no, but rather a perfectly legitimate act of government. The consequence of these changes in the American viewpoint was a Uruguay Round agreement whereby a "green light" is to be given for "assistance for research activities conducted by firms [or in institutions of] higher education or research establishments on a contract basis with firms if the assistance covers not more than 75 percent of the costs of industrial research or 50 percent of the costs of pre-competitive development activity." The agreement details permissible costs as follows:

(i) personnel costs (researchers, technicians and other supporting staff employed exclusively in the research activity);

(ii) costs of instruments, equipment, land and buildings used exclusively and permanently (except when disposed of on a commercial basis) for the research activity;

(iii) costs of consultancy and equivalent services used exclusively for the research activity, including bought-in research, technical knowledge, patents, etc.;

(iv) additional overhead costs incurred directly as a result of the research activity;

(v) other running costs (such as those of materials, supplies and the like), incurred directly as a result of the research activity.[2]

2. Agreement on Subsidies and Countervailing Measures from the Final Act Embodying the Results of the Uruguay Round of Multilateral Trade Negotiations, December 15, 1993, part iv, article 8.2A, in GATT (1994, pp. 274–75).

Compared with the permissible levels of government subsidies set in an earlier (1991) draft agreement, those under the present statement are doubled for precompetitive development activities and increased by half for "basic research." Indeed, the adjective "basic" is not used, and the definition of the activity has been altered significantly to a more applied commercial orientation. In addition, the cutoff for activity that governments are permitted to fund has been expanded to include the creation of the first noncommercial prototype. More specifically, the code defines research subsidies as follows:

—the term "industrial research" (formerly basic industrial research) means planned search or critical investigation aimed at discovery of new knowledge, with the objective that such knowledge may be useful in developing new products, processes or services, or in bringing about a significant improvement to existing products, processes or services.[3]

—the term "pre-competitive development activity" means the translation of industrial research findings into a plan, blueprint or design for new, modified or improved products, processes or services whether intended for sale or use, including the creation of a first prototype which would not be capable of commercial use. It may further include the conceptual formulation and design of products, processes or services alternatives and initial demonstration or pilot projects, provided that these same projects cannot be converted or used for industrial application or commercial exploitation. It does not include routine or periodic alterations to existing products, production lines, manufacturing processes, services, and other on-going operations even though those alterations may represent improvements.[4]

The agreement also provides a mechanism for securing green light status through a review by a subsidies committee after notification of a program. Such notification is to be updated yearly, and the entire provision is to be reviewed after five years.

---

3. In the 1991 Draft Final Act the term "basic industrial research" was defined as "original theoretical and experimental work whose objective is to achieve new or better understanding of the laws of science and engineering as they might eventually apply to an industrial activity."

4. Agreement on Subsidies and Countervailing Measures, part iv, article 8.2A in GATT (1994, p. 274).

It will no doubt be extremely difficult to get explicit, meaningful, binding rules regarding government research subsidies. Indeed, the issue is so contentious even within the United States that it threatens to hold up confirmation of the entire Uruguay Round.[5] For one thing, differences across industries are so great that rules for one may make no sense for others. For another, "national security" can be used as a reason for avoiding discipline, even though this is not explicitly recognized in the new World Trade Organization code. And, of course, governments differ with respect to their views on high-tech industrial policy, although these differences have narrowed with the changes initiated by the Clinton administration.

Nonetheless, over the foreseeable future fiscal constraints in most countries will make some less eager to launch subsidy wars such as those in the agricultural disputes of the 1980s. Furthermore, the OECD work in the field of innovation policy provides a basis for some agreement on definitions. For more than thirty years, the OECD Directorate for Science, Technology and Industry has developed and refined extremely detailed definitions that can be used to collect information on the measurement of human and financial resources devoted to R&D.[6] Some countries also use these same definitions for income tax regulations as well as for analytical and evaluation purposes. The OECD definitions and methodology should form the basis for the WTO Subsidy Committee reviews, data collection, and the WTO dispute settlement procedure. Indeed, just as science advisory groups may be called in to provide relevant information regarding disputes over the environment, it might be useful to consider an expert group on innovation policy issues, should the need arise (as it is likely to do) in the fractious area of R&D subsidies in future years. Although this proposal may not solve all the difficult and complex definitional issues, it would promote constructive, plurilateral debate and perhaps foster progress on eventual harmonization, while helping to constrain serious bilateral and unilateral destabilizing friction.

5. Senator Danforth and others argue that the new subsidy code will require the United States to match or exceed foreign subsidies and thus undertake a massive new industrial policy. See "Danforth Says . . . Force U.S. to Subsidize," *Inside U.S. Trade*, January 28, 1994, pp. 5–6.

6. The *Frascati Manual*, developed by the OECD Directorate for Science, Technology and Industry. The manual is frequently revised and refined under the guidance of country experts and the OECD secretariat.

RESEARCH CONSORTIA. As noted in chapter 2, research consortia jointly funded by the government and private institutions along the lines of Sematech or JESSI and similar Japanese projects are likely to remain a standard feature of domestic high-tech policies in the triad. A key—and unsettled—question concerns the membership of foreign subsidiaries in such consortia. Different practices in different countries have already created considerable friction, and since foreign investment and technology flows are interrelated and are likely to continue increasing, a harmonization of membership rules for consortia should be negotiated as expeditiously as possible. Such negotiations could be launched in the same OECD forum suggested above and then, at an appropriate time, transferred to the WTO for broader application.

There are no formal guidelines for participation in EU projects governed by the Commission Framework Program on technology projects. But membership in consortia are negotiated on a case-by-case basis and the "unofficial" conditions that broadly govern foreign subsidiary access to technology consortia are as follows: the research must be carried out in Europe; therefore the firm must have R&D facilities in a member country; and the first commercial application of any technology emanating from the program must be carried out in Europe. The same criteria appear to be applied in the Eureka program, which is funded by national governments and the European Union and is open to other Western European countries and not just EU members.

In the United States participation by foreign subsidiaries of multinationals is proscribed both in Sematech and in the "automobile partnership" launched by President Bill Clinton in September 1993. Other government-sponsored technology programs do not prohibit foreign participation but condition such participation on *reciprocity*, that is, on how U.S. companies are treated in the home country of the firm, as well as other factors such as market access for U.S.-owned firms and protection of intellectual property rights.[7] Thus the competitiveness concerns of the 1980s have led to the introduction of "conditional national treatment" for investment in the United States.

---

7. Some or all of these conditions are included in the National Cooperative Research and Production Act of 1993; the 1993 Defense Appropriations Act, which provides authorization and funding for the Technology Reinvestment Project; and the American Technology Preeminence Act of 1991.

In contrast, Japan's consortia have shifted their orientation toward a more basic research in recent years and have also taken steps to encourage more international participation. Indeed, the term *techno-globalism* was coined in Japan to signal this "new look."[8] This move has been widely criticized as more rhetoric than reality, especially by the United States. Certainly, such consortia are becoming less important in Japan than they were in the past and the bulk of Japanese R&D funding comes from the private sector. Nonetheless, Japan is aware of the growing criticism of the asymmetry of access for both investment and technology as compared with access in the United States and Europe. Hence a clear policy orientation on both consortia membership and international collaboration would be warranted at this time.

Thus, not only would R&D subsidies in general be useful, but it would be worthwhile to try to achieve a degree of harmonization regarding the rules for participation of foreign-owned firms in government-subsidized research consortia. Here there is probably a good chance that the United States can move toward the European policy of, in most cases, allowing firms with a research and production operation in the region into the consortium. However, the possibility of traditional national treatment seems unlikely, and therefore a limited notion of reciprocity—in the sense of acceptance of mutually agreed rules on membership and intellectual property rights—would be more feasible. Although there will be exceptions to such a rule, for example, when a country raises a "national security" issue, we think that such a norm is worthwhile and is achievable.

INTELLECTUAL PROPERTY RIGHTS. In certain areas there is ample reason to be skeptical about trying to get national policies to be similar. However, there is also much to be gained if the major industrial nations moved cautiously and thoughtfully toward greater similarity in the laws and policies associated with intellectual property rights. In fact, such convergence has already begun to take place.

There are some good reasons for trying to make national intellectual property rights laws more consistent with each other. The most important one is that it would greatly simplify international business and reduce transaction costs if companies and other inventors were

8. See *Japan Economic Institute Report* (1992).

able to deal with one basic legal code rather than a collection of codes with significant differences from country to country.

As for the arguments about leveling the playing field, most of these are complaints by nations whose companies are in the forefront of technology against countries that are lower down in the technology pecking order, with the former accusing the latter of not respecting their intellectual property rights. Although there is something to this complaint, the mutual advantages of harmonization should be the principal goal guiding international efforts in this area. It would be a mistake to focus too much attention on the complaints of the leading technological nations about the laws and policies of the lagging ones. The United States has been the principal such complainer, and it would be a grievous mistake to adopt the American point of view that the principal thing that needs to be done is for other countries to strengthen their intellectual property rights laws. "Strengthening" is a simplistic view of what the objectives ought to be.

Nor do the categories "strong intellectual property rights" and "weak intellectual property rights" characterize adequately the prevailing differences across nations in their property rights laws. The United States currently awards patents to "the first to invest," whereas all of the other major industrial nations award patents to "the first to file." In most of Europe and in Japan, patent applications are made open to the public and other parties to ensure their evidence is heard before a decision is made. Some countries of Europe and Japan also have provisions for compulsory licensing of patents under certain circumstances. In the United States compulsory licensing exists mainly as a remedy put forth after an antitrust case. The European nations distinguish inventions in terms of the inventive step involved and grant stronger and longer patent protection for inventions that represent a large step forward than for those that represent a small step. The United States has no such provisions.

Many patent lawyers seem to think that without strong patent protection firms or private inventors would have no incentive to invent. In fact, however, numerous studies have provided strong evidence indicating that the elimination of patent protection would have little effect on R&D in a large number of industries. Thus in industries like aircraft, aircraft engines, computers, semiconductors, and many others, the evidence is that the natural lead time of an innovator is the principal reason that innovation pays, and the availability of patent protection does not add much. The industries producing fine chemical products and pharmaceuticals in particular, are exceptions. Here patent protection almost surely is necessary for companies to have incentive to do R&D. It is not surprising, therefore, that representatives of these industries have been the strongest and most vocal advocates of strengthened intellectual property rights. But for many high-tech industries patent protection is but a small part of the incentives that draw forth R&D aimed at creating new products and processes.

Of course, a central argument of this essay is that lead times in many areas are shrinking, and the number of companies capable of imitating quickly has grown. In particular, the number of countries housing technologically sophisticated companies has expanded greatly. Much of the friction relating to intellectual property rights is associated with the rise of new industrial powers. Thus American firms that over the years adopted a policy of not enforcing patents or cross-licensing them with their American peers became upset when Japanese firms rose to prominence in their industries, clearly taking advantage of American creative technology. Once Japan moved to the forefront and economies like Korea and Taiwan began to develop rapidly, Japanese firms that earlier were somewhat passive about enforcing their intellectual property rights, grew more aggressive.

However, strong intellectual property rights in a field can cause difficulty for leading firms, as well as those aiming to catch up. In many technologies, the intellectual property rights associated with a broad process, or a broad product configuration, tend to be spread out among a number of companies. When patents are strongly enforced and costly to license, no company may be in a position to design and produce the best possible product without courting lawsuits. This is the reason why, in many industries, intellectual property rights have been shared, or not strongly enforced.

The growing importance in high-technology industries of international trade and multinational operation of firms has significantly increased the transaction costs of dealing with a number of different national intellectual property rights systems. There is every reason to try to harmonize better. But there also is every reason to avoid buying into the argument that harmonization means strengthening. In some cases it does, and in some cases it does not.

Trade-related intellectual property rights issues were high on the agenda of the Uruguay Round. And the negotiations there managed to cobble together an agreement. A central element of that agreement, and one that merits strong endorsement, is that all nations should adopt a principle regarding intellectual property regimes in which *foreign firms and national ones are treated alike,* except for certain special cases. By and large, however, the negotiators did not succeed in achieving much in the way of harmonization, except in the area of computer software and semiconductor chip design. It is interesting, and noteworthy, that although the negotiators agreed that all nations should treat computer programs as copyrighted material, many in the United States have recently argued that copyright protection is a very awkward way of doing the job. Similarly, concerns have been expressed that the U.S. way of protecting integrated circuit design, which is implicitly accepted in the Uruguay agreement, will not do the appropriate job for very long. In short, whenever there was agreement on a particular common standard, it is not at all clear that the right one was achieved.

Nevertheless, greater harmonization of intellectual property rights law across at least the major industrial nations is a goal worth pursuing. Most of the issues there can be resolved in negotiations between the United States and Europe, on the one hand, and the United States and Japan, on the other. In many cases, the reforms ought to involve the U.S. law, rather than the law abroad. There are signs that U.S. policymakers see it that way too. Thus the United States has made noises about adopting a first-to-file system. Particularly with the patenting of computer software, many Americans want to see a more open process of evaluating the patent application, so that the United States would look more like Europe in that regard. As for the licensing of software and several other kinds of technology, it has been suggested that United States, like Europe and Japan, ought to adopt a compulsory licensing clause regarding patents that block the use of other patented technology.

Which of these proposals should be adopted is not yet clear, and the discussions should continue. They can proceed on the basis of bilateral, or trilateral, bargaining and then be extended on a conditional most favored nation basis to other countries that agree to accept the standard. Above all, the objective of harmonization ought to be defined in terms of reducing transaction costs, rather than strengthening intellectual property rights regimes.

Mutual Recognition: Standards and Government Procurement

Although harmonization is one route to deeper integration, it is far and away the most difficult and, in a sense, intrusive. Another, based on the model of the European Union, is *mutual recognition* of different national approaches. This is also a difficult route by which to achieve concord, but it is appropriately pursued in a number of areas, the chief of which are standards and regulations that specify the characteristics of products.[9] As was seen in the HDTV example, standards in some high-tech sectors can be used as an instrument of industrial policy to try to secure a strategic advantage for a country and its corporations. Furthermore, standards setting by firms can be a competitive weapon to gain advantage over rivals. More broadly, as the GATT Code on Technical Barriers to Trade recognizes, and as the MOSS negotiations between the United States and Japan illustrate, differing standards in many high-tech sectors, especially where government procurement is involved, have been and will continue to be a source of international friction. Before turning to standards, it is useful to point out the linkage with procurement.

Government procurement for high-tech products should be tackled by a separate negotiation in the WTO on a conditional most favored nation basis. But as the MOSS experience illustrates, the codes of behavior that would govern the action of government agents for many high-tech products would not be adequate to avert international conflict if acceptable norms of performance are not established. For some of these products, an internationally funded performance center could be established to develop technical standards for performance evaluation. (The experience of the European Union's program of prenormative research should provide valuable insight in this respect.[10]) Such a performance approach would not only reduce friction but would also significantly reduce the transaction costs of national testing and certification, as well as capture economies of scale in complex areas of assessment. One should not underestimate the difficulties of an international performance

9. For a full review of the standards issue, see Sykes (1995).

10. For an American proposal on supercomputers, see *Business Week* (1993, p. 83). Note, too, the development of semiconductor equipment that Sematech has provided a central funding and testing organization for and performance specifications that lowers the costs of adoption by reducing duplication among manufacturers. See Grindley, Mowery, and Silverman (1994, p. 723–58).

approach, however. In the area of medical devices, for example, the much more litigious U.S. system could well preclude American cooperation.

On standards per se, the European Community concept of mutual recognition includes three distinct elements: minimal harmonization of national standards and regulation, mutual recognition of different country standards and regulation, and a mechanism for the binding settlement of disputes.[11]

What is the most difficult in these negotiations is to establish minimal harmonization or equivalence. As the EU experience illustrates, these problems arise because countries differ greatly in their approach to regulation, owing to "deeply-held national convictions about the dividing-line between market forces and government intervention."[12] These differences were probably at the root of the conflict between the United States and Japan on the role of product liability versus detailed regulation specifications. The objective of equivalence is to arrive at the minimal harmonization required to achieve agreed regulatory objectives. Mutual recognition will then be a matter of accepting nonessential differences. By giving preference to international performance criteria (developed by the internationally funded performance center proposed above), it should be possible to minimize detailed design specifications and differences in mandatory testing specifications that can act as technical barriers to access.

It would be very important to involve companies from a number of countries in the process of standard setting. The process itself is a means of diffusing technology, by providing a forum for the exchange of technical information among producers, users, and suppliers.[13] In this regard, the Uruguay Round Agreement on Technical Barriers to Trade shows a marked improvement over the previous, Tokyo Round code. In the latter, only 40 countries accepted the rules, whereas the WTO accord will cover all signatories to the agreement. More specifically, it includes a strong push for transparency, mutual recognition, and international standards, enjoining countries to "play a full part, within the limits of their resources, in the preparation by appropriate international standardizing bodies of international standards for

11. For an excellent summary of the EC approach as a model for an international code, see Pelkmans and Bohan (1992).

12. Pelkmans and Bohan (1992, p. 7).

13. The diffusion aspect is stressed by Ergas (1987).

products for which they either have adopted, or expected to adopt, technical regulations."[14]

Despite the improved prospects for reduced friction in high-tech standard setting opened up by the Uruguay Round, some deep-seated systemic differences remain within the triad. The much stronger consumer liability laws and greater litigiousness in the United States have already been noted. But there is also another significant difference between, for example, the United States and the European Union: far fewer American companies participate in international standards organizations. The United States has no dominant national institutions, only thousands of industry and local government organizations that create complex structural impediments to market access.[15] Indeed, the multitude of standards institutes financed by industry are not even required to notify the American National Standards Institute. Leading companies in some sectors in effect determine the product standard. This "privatization" of standard-setting policy in the United States is likely to change very slowly, so one may well expect continued bilateral negotiations and disputes in the high-tech area, especially in sectors where technological change is rapid and corporate rivalry fierce.[16]

14. Uruguay Round Agreement on Technical Barriers to Trade, Article 2.6, from Final Act Embodying the Results of the Uruguay Round of Multilateral Trade Negotiations, December 15, 1993, in GATT (1994, p.140).

15. According to the Department of Foreign Affairs and International Trade (1994, pp. 11–12), "The United States has approximately 44,000 standards jurisdictions (federal, state, and local regulatory authorities) that enforce an estimated 89,000 U.S. standards and technical regulations. This results in overlapping responsibility and redundant standards and regulations. In some cases, the products are regulated directly through inspection or testing programs, or both. In other cases, an approval body may have to certify that products meet standards set by a particular state or municipal government. This becomes a technical barrier in cases where states and municipalities have regulations that apply different standards, or where certification requirements differ.

"State regulations governing laboratory accreditation also act as barriers to trade. As stated in a National Institute of Science and Technology publication, 'Laboratories desiring to be accredited nationwide to conduct electrical safety-related testing of construction materials have to gain the acceptance of at least 43 states, more than 100 local jurisdictions, three building codes . . . , [and] a number of federal agencies, as well as several large corporations.' In other words, it is common for a testing organization to need multiple state and local government accreditation to conduct similar testing.

"The U.S. voluntary standards systems are still intact after several attempts to impose greater government control. The lack of one central standardizing body further exacerbates problems for exporters to the United States, particularly small and medium-sized companies."

16. See Woolcock (1992, chap. 6, pp. 92–110).

The proposals for harmonization and mutual recognition reviewed in the preceding paragraphs offer some hope of easing the system friction generated by global pressures for deeper integration. Even if some of these proposals were adopted over the medium term, however, such a rosy scenario would not come to grips with the other powerful pressures generating high-tech conflict in the world trading system. The most visible of these are the international spillovers of domestic regulatory policy, namely, competition policy, issues of reciprocity, and the level playing field.

International Spillovers and Reciprocity Issues

Just as there is a good case to be made for the harmonization of intellectual property laws in reducing transactions costs and leveling the playing field, there is an analogous case for competition policy, because of the broad intersect between competition policy and trade policy.[17] Thus, for example, inadequate provisions or the nonenforcement of national competition policy may restrict access to markets through imports or investment, distort trade through exemptions for export cartels, provide loopholes for market dominance at the global level because of mergers beyond the reach of national jurisdictions, and permit different standards for predatory pricing as between domestic and foreign firms (antidumping). And trade policy in the form of voluntary export restraints or voluntary import expansion may well encourage anticompetitive collusive behavior and reduce the contestability of markets.[18]

17. See OECD (forthcoming c).

18. Although we the authors agree about most matters discussed in this section, we have not reached accord on two basic matters. One is whether the conflict regarding competition and related policies is so serious that if it is not resolved it will erode the still-relatively-free world trading system and threaten the stability of its rule-based system. Ostry believes so; Nelson believes that by and large the system will endure. In the second matter, Ostry believes it essential to try to get basic operational agreement on matters on which current policies and practice are far apart. Nelson is not against trying but believes that little will be achieved. Also, he is more concerned than is Ostry that the nation that has the greatest power in such negotiations, the United States, will in some cases by pushing for policies that will reduce competition. Thus the U.S. position on "dumping" has, in his view, become downright protectionist. He worries that in many cases by "harmonization" the United States means locking in the U.S. view.

Competition policy will be high on the agenda of the new WTO, and approaches to harmonization have been explored over the past several years in the OECD and elsewhere.[19] All these studies suggest that the harmonization of competition policies, especially among OECD countries, would increase global welfare, improve efficiency, and reduce trade and investment friction.[20] But most experts also agree that harmonization will be a long and difficult process and is unlikely to be achieved over the foreseeable future.

Harmonization is difficult to achieve in competition policies for a number of reasons. Thus the overall objectives of policy vary from country to country and, indeed, have varied in the same country over time. The philosophical positions of some of the major countries involved are very different. Thus the United States, and to a lesser extent the United Kingdom, believe strongly that it is dangerous for a firm or groups of firms to possess great market power and they are particularly worried about cartels. They also pooh-pooh notions that competition can be too strong. On the other hand, the Japanese, and probably even more so the French, believe that in many cases it is desirable to encourage the growth of large firms and interfirm co-operation, and that excessive competition is a real danger. However, there seems to be some convergence among nations in these matters, with the United States moving away from its traditional strong position against cooperation between firms in the same line of business and the Europeans and the Japanese coming to place a higher value on competition than used to be the case.

Again although most countries include efficiency as an objective, only a few jurisdictions distinguish between static and dynamic efficiency. The changes in U.S. antitrust law over the 1980s designed to facilitate joint research and, more recently, joint production seem to indicate a shift in orientation toward the idea of dynamic efficiency. These differences between countries and over time reflect divergent views among experts, both economists and lawyers. There is no clear overriding consensual model in the domain of ideas. A case-by-case, fact-by-fact approach makes harmonization of any but the most gen-

19. A private group of legal experts has published an international antitrust code as a proposed plurilateral trade agreement. See Bureau of National Affairs (1993).

20. A dissenting view (that is, few gains from convergence) was expressed by the American Bar Association. See Bureau of National Affairs (1992, pp. 161–72).

eral principles acceptable. But in antitrust, perhaps more than in many other fields, the devil is in the details.[21]

Furthermore, although many countries pursue objectives other than efficiency, these social and political objectives vary across countries and may often conflict with the target of promoting efficiency. After the war many European countries granted exemptions to antitrust action to protect their weakened industries, but these exemptions have not survived under the EU competition regime. In Japan, however, the number of legal cartels is still well over 200 today, although most are to be abolished by 1995. In addition, resale price maintenance was only abolished (because of American pressure) in 1992.

Substantive convergence would be only half the battle. The variation in the enforcement of both the structural and behavioral instruments of competition policy is probably even greater than that in objectives. American pressure has certainly helped strengthen the Japanese Fair Trade Commission (FTC) (which undertook its first prosecution of a price cartel in November 1991), but the FTC has some way to go if reasonable convergence in enforcement is to be achieved among most other OECD countries. Differing legal traditions among countries are also an important factor in divergence, and the United States is unique in its emphasis on private avenues of enforcement, triple damage suits, and a greater predisposition to extraterritorial application. Differences in legal traditions among the three participants of the North American Free Trade Agreement may well impede progress in the harmonization of competition policy in order to eliminate antidumping laws. Only in the European Union has convergence been achieved, but it has taken a very long time.

One should not, of course, ignore the strong pressures for harmonization exerted by MNEs with transnational production networks. At the least, some progress on procedural issues on a bilateral or plurilateral basis in the area of mergers and joint ventures, for example, is both feasible and desirable. And, as noted above, many countries have placed competition policy high on the agenda of the new WTO. Nonetheless, to be realistic, any real progress in harmonization, substantive or procedural, will be slow to come. And thus

21. In the United States, for example, even among circuits there is disagreement on substantive matters. See Ordover and Fox (1994).

friction over competition policy in the area of trade and investment is likely to continue, especially between the United States and Japan. It is useful, therefore, to examine a few of the flashpoints and also suggest alternative approaches to mitigating friction.

One of the issues that has generated continuing friction between Japan and both the European Union and the United States concerns strategic dumping. The 1988 statement of Willy de Clerq, then head of the European Community's trade directorate, has often been cited in this regard:

> Dumping is made possible only by market isolation in the exporting country, due primarily to such factors as high tariffs or non-tariff barriers and anticompetitive practices. This prevents the producers in the importing country from competing with the foreign supplier on his own ground while allowing him to attack their domestic market by sales which are often made at a loss, or are financed from the profits made from the sale of the same or different products in a protected domestic market.[22]

More technical expositions of a similar model have been elaborated in the analysis of the U.S. color television antitrust case in which Zenith sued Matsushita for predatory pricing.[23] Strategic dumping entails subsidizing exports through higher home prices sustained by collusive price behavior and a protected home market. In industries with significant dynamic economies of scale, high fixed costs—for example, by coordinated R&D expenditure—would serve to deter entry. Thus strategic dumping is closely tied in with the exporting country's trade policy and competition policy. The injury to the importing country's firms consists of both a restriction of exports and a loss of dynamic efficiency gains (learning by doing), which may be cumulative and dispersed over a wide range of products.[24]

---

22. "Fair Practice, Not Protectionism," *Financial Times*, November 21, 1988, p. 29.

23. See Scherer, (1992, pp. 54–57). The distinction between strategic and predatory dumping rests on the issue of intent to monopolize which is included in the latter model but not in the former. See OECD (forthcoming a).

24. Although dumping involves pricing, a broader concept of technological vulnerability pertaining to the abuse of dominance by other means also raises transnational or supranational competition policy issues. See OECD (1989) and the discussion of nonprice predation (p. 83).

One way to deal with strategic dumping is for the importing country to undertake a form of harassment as a deterrent: strategic antidumping. This is likely to induce investment by the exporting firms into the importing country, as occurred during the 1980s, and thus create another set of problems. A second possibility is domestic subsidy, which would require multilateral negotiations on a new subsidy code. A third option would be to tackle the root causes of the problem, the exporting country's trade and competition policy.

To remove the barriers to access into the exporter's market, the first step would be to agree to a list of industry characteristics; for example, degree of concentration as measured by exporting firms' share of home market; exporting firms' share of world market (which would affect alternative third-country producers); extent and nature of barriers to entry of new firms or expansion of existing firms; degree of import penetration; and prices in the exporting country's home market in relation to prices elsewhere. The purpose of selecting specific industries would be to focus the negotiations on eliminating protection for sectors in which strategic behavior is feasible. These are high-tech industries, that is, sectors with oligopolistic structures, high entry barriers, significant static and dynamic efficiencies, and dominance in global markets.

From this agreed industry list one could then assemble a group of products and for these compile a list of specific import barriers. This would then form the basis for a "zero-for-zero" negotiation, that is, the removal of all border restraints on a reciprocal basis. The negotiations could begin with a small group of countries, including the United States, European Union, and Japan, and then they could decide whether the agreement should be conditional or full MFN. If conditional, the agreement should be open to all countries willing to accede to the zero tariffs.

The removal of trade barriers will not, on its own, remove the threat of strategic dumping, which also requires action on competition policy in the exporting market. Because convergence, however desirable, will be a lengthy process, a strong case could be made that in the absence of a supranational authority, bilateral agreements might be contemplated to ensure a fair hearing of disputes over enforcement where there is a charge of spillover on the trade front. The process of convergence could well be speeded up by means of transparency and international peer pressure. If this option is not pursued, extraterritoriality seems a likely alternative. Indeed, in 1992 two bills were introduced in the U.S. Senate. One would have amended the Antidumping Legislation Act to allow for the collection of triple damages by U.S. firms injured by below-cost pricing of foreign products if they can prove that foreign dumping results from "extracting profits from a closed home market." The other would have allowed firms to sue, under the Sherman Antitrust Act, those foreign companies "whose actions violate their own government's law which has not been enforced."[25] Both bills failed to pass, but new, similar bills were introduced in both the Senate and House more recently.[26]

Another competition policy issue that has so clearly emerged over the 1980s revolves around transnational mergers or, even more, transnational joint ventures in high-tech sectors. Each of the national governments may not be concerned about potential abuse of the dominant position in their own country or, indeed, each may hold different views on the matter. So disputes are likely to become more frequent. In any case, globalization logically requires a supranational authority and dispute settlement mechanism. The proposed alliance between Boeing and Airbus to produce a new 800-seat super jumbo, which would create a monopoly in this product by firms with dominant positions in competing products, is but one example of what is likely to become a more common pattern in high-technology sectors. It will be increasingly difficult for national governments that want a "piece of the action" in leading high-tech sectors to take a hard look at the global welfare implications concerning the relationship between competition and innovation. Furthermore, in many R&D alliances designed to internalize the interindustry externalities (for example, multimedia ventures), disputes over a division of the benefits are more and more likely to occur and will involve a combination of competition and intellectual property issues. No international forum now exists to handle these disputes. A supranational competition policy body could, if required, have the right to establish advisory panels to deal with on intellectual property issues. In the absence of

25. "Antitrust Chief Says Justice Dept Will Apply U.S. Law Selectively to Foreigners," *Inside U.S. Trade,* May 8, 1992, p. 8. In April 1992, the Justice Department announced that it would, in appropriate circumstances, challenge foreign business conduct that harmed U.S. exports when the conduct would have violated U.S. antitrust laws if it had occurred in the United States.

26. "House Members Press for New Attack on Anticompetitive Practices," *Inside U.S. Trade,* April 8, 1994, p. 3.

such a body, various proposals have emerged for interim bilateral or plurilateral agreements: for example, that investigative and blocking power be given to the jurisdiction in which, say, 80 percent of the sales volume is located.[27]

Another issue that emerged in the high-tech conflicts of the 1980s had to do with the notion of structural impediments to access by either exports or investment. Never precisely defined by sector or generically, the trade policy debate today nonetheless includes the concept of *effective access,* which extends the category of barriers to imports to include, in addition to tariff and nontariff barriers such as subsidies and VERs, domestic regulatory policies that are not necessarily designed to protect against imports but have that effect and other structural impediments that limit competition or transparency. A related concept, *effective presence,* refers to access via investment, which is discussed below. Effective access and presence, it is argued, are more appropriate concepts for a globalizing world in which economies of scale and scope, customization, and access to technology require broadly comparable penetration of all three triad blocs.[28] These concepts arose in the services negotiations in the Uruguay Round (which established the precedents both that domestic regulation was the major barrier to market entry and that trade and investment were alternative or complementary routes to market penetration).

The impact of the Japanese keiretsu was, as noted earlier, a recurring theme in the Structural Impediments Initiative (SII), as well as in the sectoral negotiations. The vertical production keiretsu were said to be exclusionary in the automobile sector; that is, they impeded effective access (although so does vertical integration, the enterprise model of some American companies). The United States argued that the "solution" was tougher antitrust action, but this seems rather implausible. Neither U.S. nor EU policy prohibits vertical agreements. In the European Union there are block exemptions for certain types, but the overall approach takes into account market structure as well as efficiency effects on a case-by-case basis.[29] As already noted, many studies of the automobile industry have demonstrated that

27. Ordover and Fox (1994, p. 21). For proposals on improved procedural convergence and cooperation, see OECD (1994).
28. See, for example, Feketekuty (1992).
29. See Comanor and Rey (1994).

the long-term supplier-assembler relations of the Japanese keiretsu are a more efficient organizational form than vertical integration or spot-type procurement from external suppliers. The issue of collusion should be directed at the final product market and essentially involves *horizontal* behavior. As long as competition in final products exists, the efficiency gains outweigh the exclusionary consequences. Indeed, the diffusion of the keiretsu innovation through Japanese investment in the United States and United Kingdom has improved American and British industry performance.

Although there appears to be little rationale for the use of competition policy, the exclusionary effects remain a source of friction. But these are likely to diminish over time as Japanese firms develop more transparent and inclusive procedures for intercorporate linkages.[30]

Another proposal to deal with structural impediments to effective market access that is now being debated is to bring a complaint to the WTO under a little-used section of the GATT, Article 23:1(b). The section concerns "nullification or impairment" of benefits not through violation of a specific GATT rule but through "the application by another contracting party of any measure whether or not it conflicts with the provisions of this Agreement." The European Union issued a complaint against Japan in 1983 under this broad nullification and impairment rule, which, in effect, charged that structural impediments blocked effective market access. But it subsequently withdrew the request for a panel, so the question as to whether the GATT or WTO provides a multilateral forum to handle impediments to effective access remains unanswered.[31] It would be useful to bring a

30. This is recommended by Japanese industry associations clearly as a response to American complaints. See, for example, the comprehensive analysis and proposals of the Tokyo Chamber of Commerce and Industry (1993). The vertical distribution keiretsu are much more clearly a barrier to effective access to the Japanese market, including in the automobile industry. Moreover, although there may be some efficiency gains from exclusive dealing arrangements that provide customer services and information (largely nonappropriable and therefore subject to free riding by competing distributors), such gains are outweighed by the significant exclusionary impact on imports. See Comanor and Rey (1994), who argue that it is essential to compare the efficiency gains from enhanced introbrand coordination with those from greater interbrand competition and expanded foreign trade and that "vertical restraints can retard the entry of foreign manufacturers. In that respect, the relaxed policies in recent years towards these restraints in both the United States and Japan may have artificially raised entry barriers between the two countries" (p. 26).

31. For a careful and comprehensive exposition of the possibilities of the nonviolation approach, see Hoekman and Mavroidis (1994, pp. 137–49).

complaint—say, about the impact of production keiretsu—as a test to explore the potential of the new and strengthened dispute settlement procedure of the WTO. Under these new procedures, it is possible to include experts in industrial organization and competition policy, as well as solicit information and technical advice relevant to the issue under discussion.

Although there has been a great deal of debate about impediments to effective access via exports, remarkably little attention has been paid to effective presence, via investment. This is now beginning to change, and both investment and technology issues are likely to move to the top of the international agenda in the coming years.[32]

As pointed out in chapter 1, there is a striking disparity between the inward foreign investment stock of Japan and that of Europe and the United States. The low level of foreign investment in Japan is in part a result of many decades of official restrictions, most of which were removed during the 1980s. Yet there was still an enormous disparity between the inward flows of investment to Japan and other OECD countries during the wave of transnationalization in the 1980s. As stressed in earlier discussion, trade and investment in high-tech goods are complementary routes to market penetration, and, investment is often a more effective mode for technology access. It is for these reasons that the low level of foreign investment in Japan will become central to the debate in high-tech system friction concerning the level playing field.

There are a number of reasons for the low level of foreign investment in Japan. To begin with, in the high-tech industries such as semiconductors the pre-1980 protection and industrial policy entrenched domestic oligopolies and created significant barriers to entry for both domestic and foreign firms.[33] In addition, land prices rose and costs were in general higher because of the asset price inflation at the end of the 1980s. Cost factors will continue to impede entry as the yen rises, in large part because of American policy (which is designed to improve market access). But the major *structural* impediment to effective presence is the horizontal keiretsu or, more broadly, the Japanese model of corporate governance.

---

32. For recent analyses, see Lawrence (1992, pp. 47–76); Encarnation (1992); and Mason (1992, pp. 98–115).

33. See, for example, Kimura (1993).

The intermarket, or horizontal, keiretsu, which consist of firms in diverse industries grouped around a major bank, are a fundamental aspect of Japanese capitalism.[34] The lead bank is not only an important source of capital (though less so now than in the early 1980s) but performs other functions with respect to client firms: it facilitates access to other banks, assists in restructuring if required, and provides management assistance if necessary. In addition to this long-term reciprocal relationship with the lead bank in the keiretsu, cross-shareholding is extensive among intermarket keiretsu members, although it has been eroding ever since the asset price bubble burst in the 1980s. Nonetheless, the tradition of cross-shareholding makes members resistant to takeover bids. This resistance is strengthened by the long-term stable investment strategies of insurance companies and pension funds, which also reduce the pool of publicly traded shares. This corporate governance model is thus resistant to mergers and acquisitions, the dominant mode of inward foreign investment in other countries, especially in the United States, where equity markets and other phenomena such as take-overs, shareholders' rights, and extensive disclosure regulations create active markets for corporate control. Figure 4-1 and tables 4-1 and 4-2 illustrate these differences between Japan and other countries.[35]

Is the clearly exclusionary model of corporate governance in Japan also more efficient? Is there, in other words, a parallel with the production keiretsu? A judicious answer would seem to be yes and no. A reasoned judgment suggests that the Japanese governance model and the Anglo-Saxon model are "alternatively economically rational attempts to resolve traditional universal problems of coordination and control."[36] The Japanese model seems more effective in reducing transactions costs and is particularly suited to encouraging a long view, which facilitates innovation. The Anglo-Saxon model centers on the game; the Japanese model centers on the players. An "ideal" model that would include elements of both and policy proposals to promote convergence has, indeed, been suggested by both American and Japanese experts.[37]

---

34. For a comprehensive analysis of all types of keiretsu, see Gerlach (1992).

35. There are, in fact, a large number of mergers and acquisitions in Japan, but they occur overwhelmingly among very small domestic firms. See Odagiri (1994).

36. Kester (1993, p. 1). For a similar view, see Lichtenberg and Pushner (1992).

37. See Kester (1993). In the United States a comprehensive reform of financial regulation would be required. In Japan, the bursting of the asset price bubble of the 1980s has revealed the dangers of ignoring shareholder interests. See Watanabe and Yamamoto (1992, pp. 28–45).

Figure 4-1. *Number of Mergers and Acquisitions Announced, 1984–89*

Number

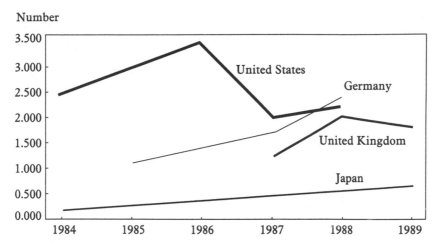

Source: Wakasugi (1993).

The convergence of governance models may be desirable and even probable, but it will not be achieved quickly. EU efforts to reduce the wide differences within Europe, the most striking of which are between the United Kingdom and Germany, have not proceeded very far. The need for corporations to raise capital in different countries may provide a stronger push to harmonization, as the Daimler Benz example suggests.[38] Nonetheless, the Japanese structural barriers to effective market presence will remain for some time to come, and other policy actions will be required to reduce the marked asymmetry.

The Japanese are now well aware of the serious nature of the deep-seated structural impediments to foreign investment in their system. The government has launched a number of projects to facilitate greenfield investment, including tax incentives to offset the high cost of land. The Keidanren issued a special report prepared by an ad hoc committee in consultation with foreign business that produced a series of recommendations involving deregulation and liberalization of key sectors, including legal services. Investment issues were included—for the first time—as one of the "baskets" in the American-

38. Waller, (1993, p. 17). The U.S. Securities and Exchange Commission is actively seeking more foreign participation. See Waller (1994, p. 19).

Table 4-1. *Japanese Merger and Acquisition Announcements, 1984–89*
Number of announced transactions

Transaction	1984	1985	1986	1987	1988	1989
Japanese purchases of Japanese firms	140	163	226	219	223	240
Japanese purchases of foreign firms	44	100	204	228	315	404
Foreign purchases of Japanese firms	6	26	21	22	19	17
Total	190	289	451	469	557	661

Source: *Japan Economic Institute Report* (1990, p. 9).

Japanese trade negotiations launched at the Tokyo Summit in July 1993.

Because mergers and acquisitions will not become a significant port of entry for foreign investment into Japan for the foreseeable future, government policy over the past few years has focused on greenfield incentives. More recently, there appears to be a shift to encouraging joint ventures. Although joint ventures are proliferating for many reasons, promoting them may provide MITI with the easiest and fastest policy response to foreign pressure.[39]

Two other investment issues have bearing on the rising international friction in high-tech: competition for "good" investment and investment-related trade measures (IRTMs). There is obviously a need for multilateral negotiations in the investment field. Although the OECD has developed investment codes and the Uruguay Round included trade-related investment measures, neither approach is fully comprehensive and both need to be expanded and updated to take into account the developments of the 1980s. A useful two-track approach could include an analysis of these issues by the OECD, which might perhaps result in an expanded code, followed by negotiations in the WTO. This two-track mode was followed, with considerable success, in the 1980s for services and the other new issues in the Uruguay Round agenda and seems the most effective way to deal with the complex nexus that has developed between trade and investment and between investment and technology.

39. See *Nikkei Weekly* (1992, p. 1); *International Trade Reporter* (1992, p. 1973).

Table 4-2. *Mergers and Acquisitions: A Comparison of the United States and Japan*

	Number		Value (billions of dollars)		Index for Japan (U.S.=1000)	
Year	United States	Japan	United States	Japan	Gross	Adjusted[a]
1985	3,490	289	146.1	0.6	4	7
1986	4,471	451	206.1	2.5	12	19
1987	4,037	489	178.3	4.9	27	44
1988	4,049	555	238.5	9.5	40	64
1989	3,766	660	245.4	13.9	57	91
1990	3,663	751	160.6	12.4	77	123
1991	2,110	614	98.2	0.4	4	7

Source: OECD (forthcoming b).
a. According to the relative GNP level.

The issue of "access to technology" has been added to the U.S.-Japan Framework talks under the heading of "economic harmonization." We have stressed the importance of diffusion of knowledge from the United States over the earlier postwar period leading to broad convergence in standards of living among the major industrialized countries by the early 1970s. We have stressed, as well, the importance of this in feeding growing American concern about "competitiveness" and increasing friction in the high-tech sectors. However, diffusion has increased significantly for the leading industrialized countries, except Japan, where the increase has been well below average (table 4-3).

In part because of the strong link between foreign investment and knowledge flows, this asymmetry of diffusion (which was assessed on the basis of patent data, an imperfect measure of a much broader concept) reflects the paucity of foreign investment in Japan. Investment is a two-way diffusion funnel. Japanese investment in Europe and the United States has served as a diffusion mechanism for enterprise innovation but also as a mechanism for providing access to American science and technology, especially through the funding of university research. To ensure that the knowledge is effectively integrated within the firm, many Japanese corporations have established R&D facilities in the United States. In the 1980s a number of R&D bases were established in Europe, in part to gain access to EU

Table 4-3. *Rate of Technology Diffusion in the G-7 Countries, 1973–90*

External/resident patent applications

Country	1973	1974	1975	1976	1977	1978	1979	1980	1981	1982	1983	1984	1985	1986	1987	1988	1989	1990
United States	1.74	1.60	1.44	1.44	1.52	1.48	1.73	1.87	2.03	1.95	2.28	2.39	2.35	2.50	2.59	2.67	2.91	3.26
United Kingdom	1.47	1.41	1.17	1.11	1.10	1.20	1.37	1.43	1.49	1.61	1.68	1.85	1.90	2.11	2.44	2.59	3.18	4.12
Japan	0.28	0.28	0.20	0.22	0.21	0.22	0.25	0.27	0.26	0.27	0.24	0.25	0.27	0.26	0.29	0.33	0.36	0.39
Germany	2.32	2.21	2.01	1.88	1.97	1.97	2.28	2.70	2.73	2.56	2.39	2.80	2.87	3.10	3.51	3.88	4.30	5.08
France	2.07	1.80	1.94	2.04	1.94	2.10	2.41	2.97	2.84	3.21	3.05	3.19	3.02	3.31	3.51	4.18	4.39	5.27
Canada	3.00	2.82	2.73	2.62	2.55	2.26	2.83	2.56	2.63	2.78	2.79	3.03	3.07	3.21	3.10	3.57	3.13	7.40
G-7 average	1.81	1.69	1.58	1.55	1.55	1.54	1.81	1.97	2.00	2.06	2.07	2.25	2.25	2.42	2.57	2.87	3.05	4.25

Sources: OECD, *Basic Science and Technology Statistics* (1991 and 1993, table 20); and OECD, *Main Science and Technology Indicators* (1993b, table 78).

Note: Comparable data for Italy were not available

technology consortia.[40] To gain access to Japan's considerable technological infrastructure, foreign firms will have to do the same. Yet few have done so. Structural barriers to investment are one factor explaining this behavior; another is the attitude of foreign firms. As an American business association official remarked:

> "The people who make decisions about where to locate R&D centers grew up in an era when the Japanese were knocking off cameras," said John P. Stern, who runs the Tokyo office of the United States Electronics Association, a trade group. "But given both the importance of the Japanese customer and Japan's increasing dominance in so many technologies, the astonishing thing is that more American companies do not see the necessity of doing R&D in Japan."[41]

But investment is not the only knowledge funnel. Technology also diffuses through trade, especially in a globalized economy in which an increasing proportion of trade is in highly sophisticated intermediate products. Estimates of the spillover effects of trade (table 4-4) show that the Japanese impact on the United States is larger than the reverse effect, although in general the U.S. spillover to other countries is still the highest. Thus Japan's main route of technological diffusion is through the export of capital goods and technically advanced components.

The Japanese are also trying to reduce international friction by encouraging foreign firms to join some government industry consortia and by pressuring private Japanese firms to open up their research facilities to foreign participants. Another policy response has been to launch two international projects, one in basic science (the human frontiers science program) and the other in precompetitive research, the intelligent manufacturing system. Serious difficulties were encountered in the launching of both, perhaps because of suspicion about Japanese motives, but also because of the lack of experience in the field of international science projects, where both the European Community and the United States have played a more active role.[42]

---

40. See Asami (1992, p. 13). In 1990 there were 119 Japanese R&D facilities in the United States and 71 U.S. facilities in Japan.

41. Sanger (1991, p. 1).

42. For an American view of the intelligence manufacturing system, see Wince-Smith (1991, pp. 25–26).

Table 4-4. *Elasticities of Total Factor Productivity with Respect to R&D Capital Stocks in the G-7 Countries, 1990*

Country	U.S.	Japan	Germany	France	Italy	United Kingdom	Canada
United States	. . .	.0203	.0036	.0013	.0005	.0022	.0022
Japan	.0237	. . .	.0007	.0003	.0001	.0003	.0001
West Germany	.0432	.0091	. . .	.0076	.0023	.0056	.0001
France	.0343	.0046	.0145	. . .	.0023	.0045	.0001
Italy	.0236	.0025	.0155	.0071	. . .	.0030	.0001
United Kingdom	.0492	.0064	.0122	.0043	.0011	. . .	.0002
Canada	.0669	.0018	.0005	.0002	.0001	.0005	. . .

Source: Coe and Helpman (1993, p. 22, table 5).

This illustrates the need for new rules for international research projects governing issues such as the sharing of costs and benefits and intellectual property rights. Today there is, in fact, a more compelling reason for such an approach than reducing international friction.

The Problem with Basic Research

This more compelling reason—although it has yet been little noticed—is that the internationalization of technology and heightened competition in high-technology industries together seem to be eroding the support of basic and long-run research programs, both private and public. While firms in high-technology industries are, in many cases, being forced to invest even more than they used to in product and process development in order to stay ahead of or up with the pack, companies that used to support significant basic research seem to be withdrawing from that. And governments seem to be shifting the portfolios of research they support toward the areas and kinds of projects that promise short-run and specific results and away from fundamental research.

Although the data are sketchy, there is considerable evidence to suggest that companies that used to invest heavily in long-run research now are drawing back. A number of American companies that had significant basic research programs during the period 1950–80 have abandoned them or have moved to make them more applied. The case of AT&T may be somewhat special, but the shortening of time horizons and the associated erosion of basic research at Bell Labs may, over the long run, lead to a significant decline in the pace of major innovation in electronics. The collapse of RCA's basic laboratory and of Xerox Park are different in some respects, but part of the same story. IBM's troubles in being able to take advantage of what comes out of its Yorktown laboratories almost surely will lead to major changes in what is done in those laboratories, perhaps at considerable cost to the evolution of computer technology.

The combination of very strong competition and less ability to prevent rivals from finding out what one is doing in research is enough to drive companies out of the basic research business. It clearly is happening in the United States. It seems to be happening in Europe. Knowledgeable observers suggest that although Japanese firms now are increasing their investments in basic and long-run research, the same problems that plagued American firms with such large investments may soon make Japanese firms think twice about the matter.

At the same time, the attention of governments has been drawn increasingly toward trying to help out their high-technology firms, often through support for research. For the most part, governments have not gotten into funding commercial product development, but the industry research they do support tends to be focused on achieving particular technological capabilities in a relatively short period of time. These glamorous new programs are not about basic and long-horizon research.

In the United States at least, the government agencies that traditionally have supported basic research at universities have been under strong pressure from Congress, and recently from the executive, to shift their funding more toward fields and projects in which relatively clear and short-run commercial benefits can be seen. And universities and government laboratories are being strongly encouraged to get closer to industry. Although less information is available on Europe, the same trends appear to be there.

More generally, there seems to be a Gresham's law at work, in which all the present inducements encourage firms, governments, and universities to shift away from basic and long-run research, and move toward research that is closer to commercialization and easier to appropriate. Thus far this problem has by and large been in electronics, but there are indications that the same problem is arising in the chemical products industry.

Many firms, and nations, in the name of competition, focus their R&D on technologies that offer clear and immediate commercial payoffs. This is a strategy designed to minimize spillover and to keep the payoffs internal. But if all firms and countries do it, the result may be a slowing down of the rate at which new understandings open up broad new technological prospects. Most of the analysis about competing industrial policies has focused on the wastefulness that such policies often involve and the international conflicts. Not much of the analysis has noted this other problem, which over the long run may be more serious.

It is a problem that calls for more coordination and cooperation than governments have thus far given it. Broader competition in high-technology fields seems inevitably to pull corporations away from basic and long-run research that they finance themselves and to reduce the ability of the companies that undertake and fund such work to take the lion's share of the benefits themselves. Governments need to respond to these developments by increasing their funding of long-run research in the relevant sciences, under one arrangement or another. Yet they seem to be shifting their research portfolios toward the applied and shorter run.

Government-financed programs that support industrial research need to put more emphasis on basic and long-run R&D. But, as is the case with company-funded basic research, there is a prisoner's dilemma here. Some intergovernmental discussions should be getting under way to try to resolve it.

Conclusions

This chapter has offered a number of policy suggestions intended to mitigate the growing system friction in the world of high-technology. They are not meant to be exhaustive: many others should be explored. But a sense of urgency is required in this endeavor, in view of the self-defeating and perverse nature of many of the high-tech national policies of the 1980s. Moreover, all policy proposals should be judged in the light of likely alternatives, especially proposals that entail unilateralism and cartelization. The price they carry in terms of world growth and equity seems far too high.

Comments

Henry Ergas

This is a broad-ranging and ambitious volume. Its sweep covers the origins and changing fortunes of the technological competitiveness of nations, the frictions between countries that is caused by shifts in competitiveness, the role of trade policy in both causing and responding to these frictions, and the scope for new initiatives aimed at strengthening international cooperation. So wide a view leaves the reader awed, and rightly so. And it makes the discussant's already difficult task more daunting than ever.

It is useful, in seeking to structure this task, to start by restating—albeit in greatly condensed and simplified form—four of the book's principal hypotheses:

—Recent years have seen the sharp erosion of U.S. technological leadership, a leadership that, having emerged in the early part of this century, peaked in the 1950s and 1960s. The main factors here have been the rise of Japanese industry as a powerful competitor in a broad range of high-technology industries, together with the increasing speed with which technology diffuses worldwide.

—Changes in technological competitiveness have created new sources of economic conflict between nations. As governments and electorates come to regard long-term wealth creation as depending on superiority in technical skills, the pressures to provide direct or indirect

Henry Ergas is a member of the Trade Practices Commission, Canberra, Australia, and visiting professor, Kennedy School of Government, Harvard University.

assistance to potential "winners" rise, creating renewed risks of trade and subsidy wars.

—At the same time, the greater speed with which technology diffuses worldwide means that firms, if they are to secure any advantage from innovation, must have ready access to foreign markets, not only through trade but also through direct investment. "Effective access" has therefore come to the fore of the policy agenda. At issue here are not only the formal restrictions to trade and investment but also, and increasingly, "structural impediments" arising from policy-sanctioned but (allegedly) exclusionary links among and between producers, distributors, and financiers.

—All of this could result in a brew as nasty as it is potent. New instruments—such as quantitative targets for imports—have been added to the protectionist's box of tricks; their acceptance by the international community has made the bully's life an easier one. Containing them requires a concerted effort to deal with the genuine sources of increased friction: in particular, the gap between a global economy, on the one hand, and stubbornly national "rules of the game," most notably for competition policy, on the other. Difficult though it may be to achieve, the harmonization of these rules is now crucial to the survival of "deep integration."

One might quibble with many of the details, but the broad picture seems eminently sensible. Clearly, we do live in an economy that is much more integrated than that of thirty years ago; and it is also one in which information, in all its forms, circulates far more quickly. The bidding away of Schumpterian rents is plausibly to the consumer's advantage; but it equally plausibly increases the uncertainty with which producers have to cope. The natural temptation is to turn to the state for insurance: both in terms of stabilized income in one's own market and of a "share of the pie" in that of others. The greater the degree to which the losers can cast the process as unfair, the more difficult it will be for governments to refuse them this insurance. Ensuring that the process not only is fair but is also seen to be so could therefore be an important part in resisting protectionist pressures.

There are, nonetheless, a few issues worth airing. These relate partly to the analysis and partly to the policy prescription.

Turning first to the analysis, I am somewhat uneasy about the picture the volume paints of the shifts in technological performance over time. Is it useful to focus, as the authors do, on trade performance in high-technology products? What these classifications mean, if anything, is debatable: Is there really anything special about producing, exporting, or importing radio sets rather than (say) machine tools? How are these categories related to economic performance and to the scope for raising living standards? It may be that these links exist, but their strength and nature is not apparent from the discussion in the volume.

Even assuming that there is some sense in which being involved in high-technology activities is desirable, is it really the case that the comparative advantage of U.S. producers in these activities has deteriorated to the extent suggested? True, U.S. firms do not have the field to themselves; but there are several areas—microprocessors, personal computers, engineering work stations, large parts of biotechnology—in which they come close to it: indeed, closer than they did a decade ago. And the picture is even sharper if one includes the service industries (noting that the boundary separating these from manufacturing is ever more blurred). Who could dispute the overwhelming strength of U.S. firms in the software industry? Certainly not the hundreds of millions of users of Microsoft's products, or the growing numbers who rely on Novell software to manage their networks, or even the vast public for ever more sophisticated forms of MTV animation. And consider the quintessential model of the activity of the future: the Internet. What is there, outside the United States, that comes vaguely close to it in scale, scope, or density?

These examples are not coincidental. Rather, they each arise from a strength of the U.S. "innovation system" that the authors mention but whose implications they do not elaborate. This is the capacity to generate and manage diversity; to provide what remains a unique seedbed for innovative entrepreneurship, reflected in vast numbers of start-up firms; and—perhaps increasingly—to interlink these firms into viable business networks consisting of autonomous component suppliers working with competing system integrators. The resulting structure is certainly less tidy than a Japanese keiretsu; but is there really any evidence that it offers a poorer vehicle for the promotion of technical advance? Clearly, the U.S. economy faces serious and deep-seated difficulties; but it is not apparent, and far from proven, that these are related to the capacity for technical innovation, at least as the term is used in this book.

This is not to say that changes in innovation performance and in the "innovation system" are irrelevant. They can have economic effects, most obviously by altering the rate of growth of productivity or inducing shifts in the terms of trade (although the authors do not provide much indication of how significant these have been). And they can also have far-reaching impacts by changing the composition, interests, and outlooks of business elites, a theme that perhaps deserves more attention than it has received in the work to date.

Consider, for example, three (perhaps caricatured) aspects of recent trends in the U.S. corporate structure: smaller size of firms; shorter corporate life cycles; and greater reliance on services than on manufacturing as a primary source of competitive advantage (even within manufacturing firms). Domestically, these features translate into a business elite even more fragmented than it has been in the past, and hence even less capable of grasping the nettle of complex social and economic issues. Externally, they help shift the policy agenda:

—Given their size and the nature of their activities, these firms will naturally attach considerable importance to issues of intellectual property.

—Being service-oriented, they will rely more heavily on foreign investment and strategic alliances than on exports to break into overseas markets.

—And quick, "effective," market access will mean more to them than to firms with longer time horizons, a greater capacity to outspend well-established rivals, and a lower reliance on independent distributors.

It is consequently wrong to believe that the new U.S. trade policy reflects the interests of yesterday's industries; rather, what may make it especially dangerous is that it so closely echoes the strengths and weaknesses of a new corporate structure. It may well be that the issues it focuses on—technological rivalry between states, effective market access, and foreign enforcement of competition policy—are actually fairly secondary to economic performance; but it is easy to see why they would appeal to an elite that, compared with its predecessors, is more imbued with the mystique of technology, more conscious of (and oriented to) world markets, and more likely to be engaged with (or look up to) firms that are relatively small or new.

The fact that the agenda has broad appeal is not, however, enough to make it worthwhile. I have suggested above that there is not much evidence that the problems it tackles are those that really matter; but there are also doubts as to whether its goals are feasible. Take the harmonization of competition policy, on which the authors lay great stress: this has proved extraordinarily difficult even within the supranational structure of the European Union; how much could really be achieved in a much looser context such as the World Trade Organization? The volume seems far more sanguine about these prospects than the other evaluations carried out to date.

In short, the arguments advanced in the book need to be qualified in a number of respects. The analysis of the relation between innovation systems, on the one hand, and differences in economic performance among industrialized countries, on the other, needs to be placed on a firmer basis. The view of the United States as a "declining hegemon" is at best questionable. The domestic roots of U.S. foreign economic policy deserve closer attention. And if —having done all of this—the clash of "technoglobalism" and "technonationalism" does emerge as *the* problem, we are still far from having found the solutions.

References

Alic, John and others. 1992. *Beyond Spinoff: Military and Commercial Technologies in a Changing World.* Harvard Business School Press.

Archibugi, Daniele, and Jonathan Michie. 1992–93. "The Globalisation of Technology: Myths and Realities." Research Papers in Management Studies 18. Cambridge, U.K.

Asami, Shuji. 1992. "Companies Set Up Overseas R&D Bases." *Nikkei Weekly,* November 9.

Beltz, Cynthia A. 1991. *High Tech Maneuvers, Industrial Policy Lessons of HDTV.* American Enterprise Institute Press.

Bergsten, C. Fred, and Marcus Noland. 1993. *Reconcilable Differences? United States–Japan Economic Conflict.* Washington: Institute for International Economics.

Bureau of National Affairs. 1992. *Antitrust and Trade Regulation Report,* vol. 62 (February 6).

———. 1993. *Antitrust and Trade Regulation Report, Special Supplement,* vol. 64 (August 19).

Business Week. 1993. "Supercomputers: A Way to Screen Out the Hype." May 31.

Caves, Richard, H. Crookell, and P. Killing. 1983. "The Imperfect Market for Technology Licenses." *Oxford Bulletin of Economics and Statistics* 45 (August): 249–67.

Chandler, Alfred, and Takashi Hikino. 1990. *Scale and Scope: The Dynamics of Industrial Capitalism.* Belknap Press.

Chesnais, Francois. 1993. "The French National System of Innovation." In *National Innovation Systems,* edited by Richard R. Nelson, 192–229. Oxford University Press.

Clarida, Richard, and Susan Hickok. 1993. "U.S. Manufacturing and the Deindustrialization Debate." *World Economy* 16 (March): 173–92.

Coe, David T., and Elhanan Helpman. 1993. "International R&D Spillovers." National Bureau of Economic Research Working Paper 4444. Cambridge, Mass.

Comanor, William S., and Patrick Rey. 1994. "Competition Policy Towards Vertical Restraints in a Global Economy." Competition Policy in a Global Economy Project.

Cowhey, Peter F., and Jonathan D. Aronson. 1993. *Managing the World Economy: The Consequences of Corporate Alliance.* Council on Foreign Relations. New York.

Croham, Douglas. 1989. *Reciprocity and the Unification of the European Banking Market.* Occasional Papers 27. New York: Group of Thirty.

Department of Foreign Affairs and International Trade. 1994. *Register of United States Barriers to Trade, 1994.* Ottawa: 11–12.

Done, Kevin. 1993. "Carmakers Hit the Panic Button." *Financial Times,* June 17, 11.

Dunne, Nancy. 1993. "U.S. Pacts Must be 'Results-Oriented.'" *Financial Times,* June 15, 5.

Dunning, John H. 1993a. "Globalization: The Challenge for National Economic Regimes." The Geary Lecture.

Dunning, John H. 1993b. *Multinational Enterprises and the Global Economy.* Addison-Wesley.

Economic Report of the President. 1994. Washington: U.S. Government Printing Office.

Economist. 1994. "Europe's Carmakers." Vol. 330, February 5, 19–20.

Encarnation, Dennis J. 1992. *Rivals beyond Trade: America versus Japan in Global Competition.* Cornell University Press.

Ergas, Henry. 1987. "Does Technology Policy Matter?" In *Technology and Global Industry: Companies and Nations in the World Economy,* edited by Bruce R. Guile and Harvey Brooks, 191–245. Washington: National Academy Press.

Feketekuty, Geza. 1992. *The New Trade Agenda.* Washington: Group of Thirty.

Flamm, Kenneth. 1990. "Semiconductors." In *Europe 1992: An American Perspective,* edited by Gary Clyde Hufbauer, 248–57. Brookings.

———. 1993. "Semiconductor Dependency and Strategic Trade Policy." *Brookings Papers on Economic Activity, Microeconomics, I:* 249–333.

Freeman, Chris, and John Hagedoorn. 1992. "Convergence and Divergence in the Internationalisation of Technology." Paper prepared for the Merit Conference, Convergence and Divergence in Economic Growth and Technical Change, Maastricht.

General Agreement on Tariffs and Trade. Secretariat. 1994. *The Results of the Uruguay Round of Multilateral Trade Negotiations: The Legal Texts.* Geneva.

Gerlach, Michael L. 1992. *Alliance Capitalism: The Social Organization of Japanese Business.* University of California Press.

Graham, Edward M., and Paul R. Krugman. 1989. *Foreign Direct Investment in the United States.* 2d ed. Washington: Institute for International Economics.

Griffiths, John. 1994. "VW to Boost Component Orders with UK." *Financial Times,* January 25, 9.

Grindley, Peter, David Mowery, and Brian Silverman. 1994. "Sematech and Collaborative Research: Lessons in the Design of High-Technology Consortia." *Journal of Policy Analysis and Management* 13 (Fall): 723–58.

Hagedorn, John. 1990. "Organizational Modes of Inter-Firm Cooperation and Technology Transfer." *Technovation* 10 (February): 17–30.

Hoekman, Bernard M., and Petros C. Mavroidis. 1994. "Competition, Competition Policy and the GATT." *World Economy* 17 (March): 137–49.

Hudec. 1990. "Mirror, Mirror on the Wall: The Concept of Fairness in United States Trade Policy." *Proceeding of the 19th Annual Conference.* Ottawa: Canadian Council on International Law.

International Monetary Fund (IMF). 1993. *International Financial Statistics Yearbook 1993.* Washington.

International Trade Reporter. 1992. "MITI Considers Asking Japanese Firms to Encourage Foreign Tie-Ins." November 18.

———. 1993. "U.S. Again Postpones Procurement Action: E.C. Offers New Proposal Kantor Says." March 31.

Japan Economic Institute Report. 1990. No. 14A, April 6.

———. 1992. No. 28A, July 24.

———. 1993. *1993 Update on Japanese Research and Development: The Party's Over.* October 15.

Keck, Otto. 1993. "The National System for Technological Innovation in Germany." In *National Innovation Systems,* edited by Richard R. Nelson, 115–57. Oxford University Press.

Kester, W. Carl. 1993. "American and Japanese Corporate Governance Converging to Best Practice?" Working Paper. Harvard Business School.

Kimura, Yui. 1993. "Inward Foreign Direct Investment in the Semiconductor Industry in Japan." Yale University, School of Organization and Management. (May).

Krugman, Paul R., ed. 1987. *Strategic Trade Policy and the New International Economics.* MIT Press.

———. 1992. "Technology and International Competition: A Historical Perspective." In *Linking Trade and Technology Policies: An International Comparison of the Policies of Industrialized Nations,* edited by Martha Caldwell Harris and Gordon E. Moore, 13–38. Washington: National Academy Press.

Kurth, Wilhelm. 1992. "Technology and Shifting Comparative Advantage" in OECD, *Science, Technology, Industry Review,* no. 10 (April): 22.

Lawrence, Robert Z. 1992. "Japan's Low Levels of Inward Investment: The Role of Inhibition on Acquisitions." *Transnational Corporation* 1 (December): 47–76.

Levin, Richard and others. 1987. "Appropriating the Returns from Industrial R and D," *Brookings Papers on Economic Activity, 3:* 783–831.

Levy, Frank, and Richard Murnane. 1992. "U.S. Earnings Levels and Earnings Inequality: A Review of Recent Trends and Proposed Explanations." *Journal of Economic Literature* 30 (September): 1333–81.

Lichtenberg, Frank R., and George M. Pushner. 1992. "Ownership Structure and Corporate Performance in Japan." Working Paper 4092. National Bureau of Economic Research. Cambridge, Mass.

Low, Patrick. 1993. *Trading Free: The GATT and U.S. Trade Policy.* Twentieth Century Fund Press.

Maddison, Angus. 1991. *Dynamic Forces of Capitalist Development: A Long-run Comparative View.* Oxford University Press.

Mason, Mark. 1992. "United States Direct Investment in Japan: Trends and Prospects." *California Management Review* 35 (Fall): 98–115.

McKinsey Global Institute. 1993. *Manufacturing Productivity.* Auto Assembly Case Study Summary.

Mowery, D. C. 1991. "Public Policy Influences on the Formation of International Joint Ventures." *International Trade Journal* 6 (Fall): 29–62.

Mowery, David, and Nathan Rosenberg. 1993. "The U.S. National Innovation System." In *National Innovation Systems,* edited by Richard R. Nelson, 29–75. Oxford University Press.

Narin, Francis, and E. Noma. 1985. "Is Technology Becoming Science?" *Scientometrics* 7 (March): 369–81.

National Science Board. 1989. *Science and Engineering Indicators—1989,* Washington: U.S. Government Printing Office.

———. 1991. *Science and Engineering Indicators—1991,* Washington: U.S. Government Printing Office.

———. 1993. *Science and Engineering Indicators—1993,* Washington: U.S. Government Printing Office.

Nelson, Richard R. 1984. *High Technology Policies: A Five-Nation Comparison.* American Enterprise Institute.

———. 1990. "Capitalism as an Engine of Progress." *Research Policy* 19 (June): 193–214.

———, ed. 1993. *National Innovation Systems: A Comparative Study.* Oxford University Press.

Nelson, Richard R., and Gavin Wright. 1992. "The Rise and Fall of American Technological Leadership: The Postwar Era in Historical Perspective." *Journal of Economic Literature* 30 (December): 1931–64.

Nikkei Weekly. 1992. "Japan, U.S. Firms Forge Alliances to Survive." August 8.

Odagiri, Hiroyuki. 1994. "Mergers and Acquisitions in Japan and the Antimonopoly Policy." Competition Policy in a Global Economy Project.

Odagiri, Hiroyuki, and Akira Goto. 1993. "The Japanese System of Innovation: Past, Present, and Future." In *National Innovation Systems,* edited by Richard R. Nelson, 76–114. Oxford University Press.

OECD. 1989. *Predatory Pricing.* Paris.

———. 1990. *Economic Surveys, Japan 1989/90.* Paris.

———. 1991 and 1993. *Basic Science and Technology Statistics.*

———. 1992a. *Globalisation of Industrial Activities.* Paris.

———. 1992b. *Industrial Policy in OECD Countries, Annual Review, 1992.* Paris.

———. 1992c. *Science, Technology, Industry Review.* Paris.

———. 1993a. *Intra-Firm Trade.*

———. 1993b. *Main Science and Technology Indicators.*

———. 1993c. *Economic Surveys, United States 1993.*

———. 1993d. *Obstacles to Trade and Competition.* Paris.

———. 1994. *Merger Cases in the Real World: A Study of Merger Control Procedures.* Paris.

———. Forthcoming a. *Competition Policy and Antidumping.* Paris.

———. Forthcoming b. *National Systems for Financing Innovation.* Paris.

————. Forthcoming c. *Trade and Competition Policies: Objectives and Methods.* Paris.

————. Directorate for Science, Technology and Industry. *Frascati Manual.*

Oliver, Nick, and Barry Wilkinson. 1988. *The Japanization of British Industry.* Oxford: Basil Blackwell.

Ordover, Janusz, and Eleanor M. Fox. 1994. "Antitrust: Harmonization Accommodation and Coordination of Law." *Competition Policy in a Global Economy Project.*

Ostry, Sylvia. 1990. *Government and Corporations in a Shrinking World.* New York: Council on Foreign Relations.

Pelkmans, Jacques, and Niall Bohan. 1992. "Towards an Ideal GATT TBT Code?" Brussels: Centre for European Policy Studies.

Report of the Advisory Committee for Trade Policy and Negotiations. 1993. *Major Findings and Policy Recommendations on U.S.-Japan Trade Policy.*

Rutter, John. 1992. "Recent Trends in International Direct Investment." U.S. Department of Commerce.

Sanger, David E. 1991. "When the Corporate Lab Goes to Japan." *New York Times,* April 28, 1.

Scherer, F. M. 1992. *International High-Technology Competition.* Harvard University Press.

Servan-Schreiber, J. J. 1968. *The American Challenge.* New York: Athenaeum.

Siddharthan, N.S., and M. Kumar. 1990. "The Determinants of Inter-Industry Variations in the Proportion of Intra-Firm Trade: The Behaviour of U.S. Multinationals." *Weltwirtschaftliches Archiv* 126(3): 581–90.

Stoneman, Paul. 1987. *The Economic Analysis of Technology Policy.* Oxford University Press.

Sykes, Alan O. Forthcoming. *Product Standards for Internationally Integrated Goods Markets.* Brookings.

Tokyo Chamber of Commerce and Industry. 1993. *Building a New Corporate Network: Report on Research into Corporate Keiretsu.*

Tyson, Laura. 1992. *Who's Bashing Whom? Trade Conflict in High Technology Industries.* Washington: Institute for International Economics.

United Nations. *International Trade Statistics Yearbook,* Various issues.

————. 1992. *World Investment Report, 1992.* New York.

————. 1993a. *World Investment Directory. Vol. 3: Developed Countries.* New York.

————. 1993b. *World Investment Report.* New York.

U.S. Congress. 1993. Office of Technology Assessment. *Multinationals and the National Interest: Playing by Different Rules.*

————. 1993. *Survey of Current Business.* May and July.

Wakasugi, Ryuhei. 1993. "Determinants of Foreign Direct Investment in Japan." Draft of a paper presented at the Yale Conference on Foreign Direct Investment in Japan. May.

Walker, William. 1993. "National Innovation Systems: Britain." In *National Innovation Systems,* edited by Richard R. Nelson, 158–91. Oxford University Press.

Waller, David. 1993. "A Shine on Its Financial Face: Domestic and Foreign Pressures Are Forcing Reform on Germany's Capital Markets." *Financial Times,* July 14, 17.

————. 1994. "SEC Head Launches German Initiative." *Financial Times*, March 1, 19.

Watanabe, Shigeru, and Isao Yamamoto. 1992. "Corporate Governance in Japan: Ways to Improve Low Profitability. *Nomura Research Institute Quarterly* 1 (Winter): 28–45.

Wince-Smith, Deborah. 1991. "Perspectives on U.S. Technological Competitiveness." *Business and the Contemporary World* (Autumn): 25–26.

Woolcock, Stephen. 1992. *Trading Partners or Trading Blows? Market Access Issues in E.C.-U.S. Relations.* New York: Royal Institute of International Affairs and Council on Foreign Relations.

World Almanac. 1993. *The World Almanac and Book of Facts 1994*, 300–01. World Almanac.

Wyckoff, Andrew W. 1993. "The International Expansion of Productive Networks." *OECD Observer* 80 (February/March): 8–11.

Yamawaki, Hideki. 1991. "Exports and Foreign Distributional Activities: Evidence on Japanese Firms in the United States." *Review of Economics and Statistics* 73 (May): 294–300.

Index